D1220178

THE RACIAL POLICIES OF AMERICAN INDUSTRY

REPORT NO. 2

THE NEGRO IN THE AEROSPACE INDUSTRY

by

HERBERT R. NORTHRUP

Chairman, Department of Industry

Wharton School of Finance and Commerce

University of Pennsylvania

Published by

INDUSTRIAL RESEARCH UNIT, DEPARTMENT OF INDUSTRY

Wharton School of Finance and Commerce

University of Pennsylvania

Produced and Distributed by

University of Pennsylvania Press

Philadelphia, Pennsylvania 19104

Library of Congress Catalog Card Number 68-55932
MANUFACTURED IN THE UNITED STATES OF AMERICA
9041

FOREWORD

In September 1966, the Ford Foundation announced a major grant to the Industrial Research Unit of the Wharton School to fund a three-year study of the Racial Policies of American Industry. The purpose of the study is to determine why some industries are more hospitable to the employment of Negroes than are others and why some companies within the same industry have vastly different racial employment policies, and to propose appropriate policy.

The studies have proceeded on an industry-by-industry basis, under the direction of the undersigned, with Dr. Richard L. Rowan, Associate Professor of Industry, as Associate Director. In addition, both Dr. Rowan and the undersigned have undertaken specific industry studies. This study of the aerospace industry is the second in a series of reports dealing with particular industries; the first, published in January 1968, covered the automobile industry. Studies of the hotel, iron and steel, pulp and paper, petroleum, rubber tire, insurance, department store, and some fifteen other industries are scheduled to be published during the next few years. We expect during this period also to complete major studies combining and comparing the findings of the various industry studies.

Manuscript and typing assistance were provided by Mrs. Margaret E. Doyle, Mrs. Helen S. White, and Mrs. Marie P. Spence, and administrative and secretarial functions were also cared for by Mrs. Doyle. Mrs. Marjorie C. Denison and Miss Elsa Klemp did the table calculations, proofreading, and index. Errors or shortcomings, of course, are the responsibility of the undersigned.

Philadelphia
June 1968

HERBERT R. NORTHRUP

TABLE OF CONTENTS

LIST OF TABLES

LIST OF FIGURES

CHAPTER I.

Introduction

Aerospace provides the best example of how the Negro has fared in an industry which is overwhelmingly dependent upon government as its principal customer. Yet the extent of Negro employment and upgrading in the industry is affected by a number of factors other than the pressures of the prime customer, such as industrial location and skill requirements. Moreover, the pressures of the government as customer are not unilateral, but must consider besides racial employment, such significant matters as delivery dates, labor force quality as it relates to reliability and safety of product performance, and military security. As a result, a complex of governmental-customer pressures bears upon the industry's racial employment policies.

This study is concerned with the development, status, and problems involved in racial employment policies in the aerospace industry, and in the principal companies therein. Basic to an understanding of these policies is the nature of the industry which is the subject of the next section of the study.

CHAPTER II.

The Aerospace Industry

The aerospace industry is actually a vast grouping of industries and companies rather than an industry in the strict sense of the term. It is basically an outgrowth of the aircraft industry, and reflects the dynamic changes which have occurred in the reorientation of that industry to missile, space, and to advanced research and development in the manned aircraft and outerspace fields. By the very nature of the requirements for production of sophisticated manned and unmanned aircraft, companies in aerospace have developed increasing need for and competence in electronics. Several, such as United Aircraft, General Dynamics, Northrop, or Hughes, have either purchased electronics companies, have built up their own electronic divisions, or have done both. In turn, major electronic companies have become big factors in both aircraft and space development and manufacturing. Thus the General Electric Company is both one of the two major builders of jet engines and one of the leading developers and builders of space vehicles and apparatus. Radio Corporation of America and Westinghouse Electric are also large space contractors.

The manufacture of large and complicated hardware and equipment has attracted other major concerns. Chrysler is a principal fabricator of the Saturn missile; General Motors manufactures engines and components used in flight; and numerous companies, large and small, contribute to the making of manned and unmanned air and space vehicles, communication satellites, aircraft, and other items.

The capacities developed by aerospace companies and their desire to diversify have led them into nonaerospace ventures. Lockheed Aircraft purchased and now operates a shipbuilding concern; General Dynamics operates shipyards, an electronics firm, and a host of other businesses. In 1967 North America Aviation merged with Rockwell-Standard, a conglomerate company primarily in nonaerospace operations.

The complexities of the industry, therefore, do not lend themselves to easy statistical collection, especially since the mid-1950's and the development of the outerspace research and exploration programs, which required new hardware, techniques, and company

TABLE 1. *Employment in Standard Industrial Classifications of the Aerospace Industry*
1958 and 1963

SIC No.	Industry	1958	1963
37211	Complete aircraft, military type	322,079	147,763
37214	Modifications, conversions and overhaul of aircraft	17,485	29,683
37216	Other aeronautical services for aircraft	9,717	72,947
37221	Aircraft engines for U. S. military	n.a.	66,618
37223	Research and development on aircraft engines	33,488	7,552
37224	Aircraft engine parts and accessories	63,185	39,227
37225	Complete missile or space vehicle engines and/or propulsion units	n.a.	17,716
37226	Research and development on complete missile or space vehicle engines and/or propulsion units	n.a.	51,773
37228	Missile and space vehicle engines and/or propulsion units parts or accessories	n.a.	5,377
37291	Other aircraft parts and auxiliary equipment	195,027	106,799
37292	Guided missile components and subassemblies, n.e.c.	n.a.	40,267
37293	Research and development on aircraft parts	n.a.	1,159
37294	Research and development on missile parts and components, n.e.c.	n.a.	21,990
38111	Aircraft flight, nautical, and navigational instruments and automatic pilots	45,957	15,490
38211	Aircraft engine instruments, except flight	1,256	5,299
	Total	688,194	629,660

Source: *Compendium of Manufacturing Production Statistics for the United States, 1947-1965* (Washington, D. C., Georgetown Economic Data Library, Georgetown University, 1967), pp. 264-268.

capabilities. The governmental standard industrial classification system (SIC) now recognizes a variety of divisions in the industry, as set forth in Table 1, with the employment for 1958 and 1963. These data, however, greatly understate the numbers of people involved who are subject to the policies of aerospace companies and work directly in, or closely related to, basic aerospace activity.

Since the prime purpose of this study is an analysis of an industry's racial policies, and those of its major component companies, the data developed by the Aerospace Industries Association of America, Inc., more accurately reflect the numbers of employees who are affected by aerospace company policies. The Association data are based upon both government statistics and direct reports from the companies to the Association, and are utilized here to describe the industry for the purposes of this study.

In terms of company policies, emphasis in this study will be on those concerns which are primarily aerospace. Thus although some employment data of Chrysler or General Electric, for example, will undoubtedly be included in the general aerospace figures, discussions of policies of such companies, or those similarly situated, will be found in other monographs in this series dealing with the automobile or electrical and/or electronic industries respectively.[1]

SALES AND STRUCTURE

The aerospace industry, as defined herein, is the largest manufacturing industry in the United States. The Aerospace Industries Association, Inc., reported that in 1966, total sales of the aerospace industry reached a post-World War II high of 24.2 billion, and that 2 billion of these sales were of nonaerospace products sold by the

TABLE 2. *Aerospace Sales and the National Economy 1960-1966*

(Billions of Dollars)

Year Ending December 31	Total Gross National Product	Sales of Manufacturing Industries	Sales of Durable Goods Industry	Sales of Aerospace Industry	Aerospace Sales as Percent of GNP	Aerospace Sales as Percent of Manufacturing Industries	Aerospace Sales as Percent of Durable Goods
1960	503.7r	369.6	189.8	17.3	3.4	4.7	9.1
1961	520.1r	370.6	186.4	18.0	3.5	4.9	9.7
1962	560.3r	399.7	206.2	19.2	3.5	4.8	9.3
1963	590.5r	417.5	217.0	20.1	3.4	4.8	9.3
1964	631.7r	445.6	230.8r	20.6r	3.3	4.6	9.0
1965	681.2r	483.3r	252.2r	20.7r	3.0	4.3	8.2
1966	739.6	528.4	276.1	24.2	3.3	4.6	8.8

r Revised.

Sources: Manufacturing and Durable Goods Industries: Department of Commerce, U. S. Bureau of Census, *Manufacturers' Shipments, Inventories, and Orders, Series M-3.*

Gross National Product: U. S. Department of Commerce, *Survey of Current Business.*

Aerospace: Aerospace Industries Association estimates, based on latest available information.

Data compiled by Aerospace Industries Association.

1. See Herbert R. Northrup, *The Negro in the Automobile Industry* (Philadelphia: University of Pennsylvania, Industrial Research Unit, 1968) The Racial Policies of American Industry, Report No. 1. The study on the electrical and electronic industries is still in preparation.

industry from plants where aerospace manufacturing or research was the prime business. According to this same source, aerospace sales in 1966 were 3.3 percent of gross national product, 4.6 percent of manufacturing sales, and 8.8 percent of durable goods sales.[2] Table 2 summarizes the industry's sales data for the years 1960-1966.

Table 3 lists the twelve largest companies whose principal products are in the aerospace industry as of 1966. Two-thirds of them are billion dollar sales companies and seven have more than 50,000 employees. Mergers subsequent to 1966 have increased the size of several of these companies. Such giants as General Electric Company, Radio Corporation of America, Textron, and Westinghouse Electric undoubtedly have aerospace product sales and employment equal to, or greater than, some of the companies listed here but companies do not publish data by product or divisions.

The industry is one which is dominated by large corporations,

TABLE 3. *Sales and Number of Employees Twelve Major Aerospace Companies, 1966*[1]

Company	1966 Sales[2] (000 Dollars)	Employees[2] 1966	Headquarters City
Boeing	2,356,567	128,500	Seattle
Lockheed Aircraft	2,084,759	90,355	Burbank, Cal.
North American Aviation[3]	2,023,782	92,150	El Segundo, Cal.
General Dynamics	1,796,991	93,196	New York
United Aircraft	1,663,203	81,556	East Hartford, Conn.
McDonnell[4]	1,060,039	44,285	St. Louis
Grumman Aircraft Engineering	1,059,379	34,500	Bethpage, N. Y.
Douglas Aircraft[4]	1,048,012	80,200	Santa Monica, Cal.
TRW	863,866	58,827	Cleveland
Martin-Marietta	669,821	32,000	New York
Avco	604,220	35,000	New York
Ling-Temco-Vought[5]	468,251	26,158	Dallas

1. This list includes those whose principal products are aerospace. Thus General Electric, Radio Corporation of America, Textron's Bell subsidiary, General Tire's Aerojet-General subsidiary, etc. are not included although their aerospace sales and employment may exceed those of companies listed here.
2. Include both aerospace and nonaerospace figures.
3. Merged with Rockwell-Standard in 1967.
4. McDonnell and Douglas merged in 1967, under McDonnell control and leadership.
5. Merged with several nonaerospace concerns in 1967.

Source: *The Fortune Directory,* June 15, 1967.

---

2. The Aerospace Industries Association of America, Inc., publishes an annual book, *Aerospace Facts and Figures.* These data are found in the 1967 edition.

although many small concerns provide needed services and products. The tremendous investment in research, engineering, plant and equipment, in manpower, services and management, even granting government support, are such that small concerns cannot compete

FIGURE 1. *Sales of the Aerospace Industry by Customer*

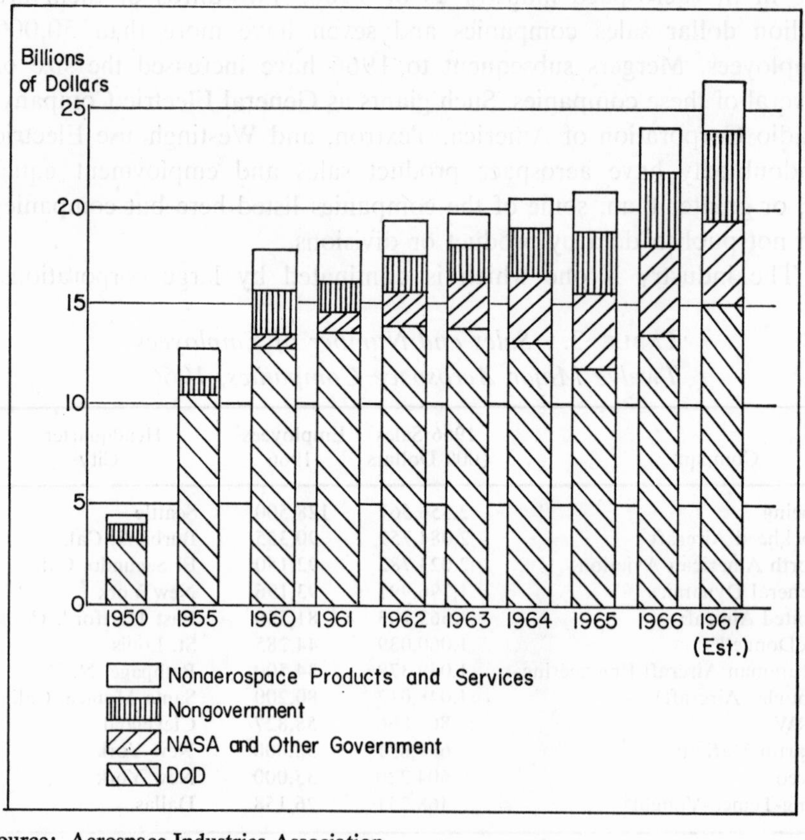

Source: Aerospace Industries Association.

for the major contracts. The difficulties encountered by General Dynamics, in the early 1960's, and by Douglas, more recently,[3]

3. The Convair Division of General Dynamics lost so much money on the 880 and 990 planes that the Corporation reported in successive years, the two greatest losses in American corporate history. There resulted a thorough reorganization and management upheaval. Douglas ran out of funds, probably as a result of poor estimating and poorer management controls in 1966-67, despite an excellent order backlog, and was forced to merge with McDonnell, which now is in control of the joint operation.

emphasize the managerial and investment problems inherent in the industry.

The governmental interest in the industry is shown by the data in Figure 1. Almost three-fifths of the industry's sales were absorbed by the Department of Defense, about another fifth by the National Aeronautical and Space Agency, with the balance divided between nongovernmental customers, and customers for nonaerospace products and services produced in aerospace plants. Obviously, the industry must give careful heed to governmental policies and programs, including racial employment policies which are part and parcel of every government contract.

The industry-government relationship is further emphasized by Table 4 which lists the twelve largest defense contractors in 1967. Of these, only four—General Electric, American Telephone and Telegraph, General Motors, and Textron—are not primarily aerospace concerns. As already noted, General Electric has large aerospace divisions, and General Motors is also active in the field. American Telephone and Telegraph is a large producer and servicer of aerospace communications, and Textron's divisions include Bell Helicopter and Bell Aerosystems.

TABLE 4. *The Twelve Largest Defense Contractors by Volume of Defense Orders, 1967*

Company	Volume (Millions of Dollars)	1966 Rank
1. McDonnell-Douglas Corp.	2,125	*
2. General Dynamics Corp.	1,832	4
3. Lockheed Aircraft Corp.	1,807	1
4. General Electric Co.	1,290	2
5. United Aircraft Corp.	1,097	3
6. Boeing Company	912	5
7. North American Aviation, Inc.	689	10
8. American Telephone & Telegraph Co.	673	7
9. General Motors Corp.	625	11
10. Ling-Temco-Vought, Inc.	535	22
11. Textron, Inc.	497	8
12. Grumman Aircraft Engineering Corp.	488	21

* McDonnell and Douglas merged in 1967. In 1966 McDonnell ranked 6th, Douglas 24th.

Source: U. S. Department of Defense data, reproduced in *Business Week*, December 9, 1967, p. 152.

The product breakdown of the industry's sales is shown in Figure 2. The industry was once almost totally concerned with aircraft, but recently about 50 percent of its product sales dollars are in missiles or space vehicles—products which did not exist before 1950. In addition, of course, the modern turbojet, subsonic and supersonic aircraft are far more complicated and sophisticated than the piston

FIGURE 2. *Sales of the Aerospace Industry by Product*

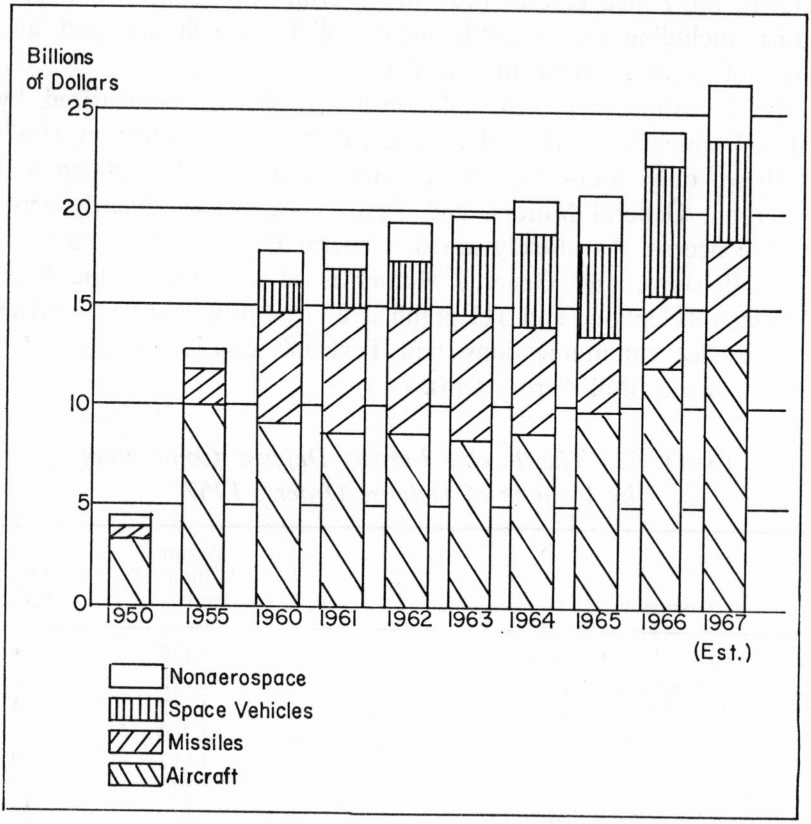

Source: Aerospace Industries Association.

engine planes which dominated military and civilian aviation until recently. The heavy input of a small number of numerous types of missiles, space vehicles, and high-speed manned aircraft, as compared with building a smaller variety of less complicated aircraft in large numbers, profoundly affects the labor force requirements of the industry. As we shall note, this adds problems for Negro employment by requiring even higher skills in the face of the fact that such skills are disproportionately absent from the Negro community.

MANPOWER

Employment and payrolls in the industry reflect these gigantic sales data. In 1966, the industry reported an average employee force of 1,298,000 and average annual payrolls of 11.2 billion dollars. Employment in the industry was respectively 6.8 percent of all manufacturing employment and 8.8 percent of all manufacturing payroll.[4] Today, one out of every 15 employees in manufacturing is employed in the aerospace industry. Table 5 summarizes employment and payroll data, 1959-1966.

The data in Table 5 also reveal another characteristic of the industry—the large percentage of salaried employees. Since 1960, the salaried payroll has consistently exceeded the hourly one, and the numbers of salaried employees have been almost equal to, or in some

TABLE 5. *Employment and Payroll in the Aerospace Industry, 1959-1966*

Year Ending December 31	Employment (Annual Average in Thousands)			Payroll (Annual Average in Millions of Dollars)			Aerospace as Percent of Total	
	Total	Salaried	Production workers	Total	Salaried	Production workers	Manufacturing employment	Manufacturing payroll
1959	1,128	455	673	7,427	3,692	3.735	6.8	8.5
1960	1,074	467	607	7,317	3,835	3,482	6.1	8.2
1961	1,096	499	597	7,809	4,257	3,552	6.7	8.7
1962	1,177	558	619	8,889	5,045	3,844	7.0	9.2
1963	1,174	594	580	9,102	5,421	3,681	6.9	9.0
1964	1,117	565	552	8,897	5,326	3,571	6.5	8.3
1965	1,133	562	571	9,502	5,429	4,073	6.2	8.2
1966	1,298	612	686	11,235	6,061	5,174	6.8	8.8

Sources: Manufacturing Employment: U. S. Bureau of Labor Statistics, *Employment and Earnings.*
Manufacturing Payroll: U. S. Bureau of Employment Security—Office of Business Economics estimates.
Aerospace Employment and Payroll: Aerospace Industries Association, based on latest available information.
Data compiled by Aerospace Industries Association.

4. See note 2, above.

TABLE 6. *Scientists and Engineers in Research and Development Total and Aerospace Industry, 1957-1966*

As of January	Total	Aircraft and Missiles	Aerospace as a Percent of Total
1957	229,400	58,700	25.6
1958	243,800	58,600	24.0
1959	268,400	65,900	24.6
1960	292,000	72,400[r]	24.8[r]
1961	312,100	78,500[r]	25.2[r]
1962	312,000	79,400[r]	25.4[r]
1963	327,300	90,700[r]	27.7[r]
1964	340,200	99,400[r]	29.2[r]
1965	343,600	97,400[r]	28.3[r]
1966	358,900	100,700	28.1

Note: Scientists and engineers working less than full time have been included in terms of their full-time-equivalent number.

[r] Revised.

Source: National Science Foundation.

Data compiled by Aerospace Industries Association.

years in excess of, the number of production workers. One reason for this is the tremendous research and development effort in the industry. Table 6 shows that the number of scientists and engineers employed in the industry have averaged about one-fourth of those in the country since 1957.

In addition to scientists and engineers in research and development, the aerospace industry requires huge clerical, accounting, finance, personnel, systems and computer and data processing staffs to operate and to control its manufacturing, research, and testing facilities. The significance of clerical, technical, engineering and scientific personnel in the industry has, of course, a distinct impact on the industry's capacity to employ Negroes, since Negroes are disproportionately unrepresented among these groups in our society.

The changing importance of missiles and space vehicles in the industry's employment picture is shown in Table 7. In 1962-1963, employment in this branch of the aerospace industry exceeded that in the traditional aircraft industry. This is significant for Negro labor trends because aircraft manufacturing requires a much higher percentage of production work. For example, in 1966, about two-thirds of those employed in aircraft were production workers, whereas only one-half of those in missile and space employment were so classified.

TABLE 7. *Estimated Sales of the Aerospace Industry by Product Group, 1948-1967*

(Millions of Dollars)

Year Ending December 31	Total Sales	Product Group			
		Aircraft	Missiles	Space Vehicles	Non-aerospace
1948	1,493	1,359	—	—	134
1949	2,232	2,032	—	—	200
1950	3,116	2,731	105	—	280
1951	6,264	5,067	633	—	564
1952	10,130	8,442	776	—	912
1953	12,459	10,420	918	—	1,121
1954	12,807	10,460	1,194	—	1,153
1955	12,411	9,781	1,513	—	1,117
1956	13,946	10,485	2,206	—	1,255
1957	15,858	11,398	3,033	—	1,427
1958	16,065	10,582	4,036	1	1,446
1959	16,640	9,714	5,042	386	1,498
1960	17,326	9,126	5,762	878	1,559
1961	17,997	8,847	6,266	1,264	1,620
1962	19,162	8,944	6,311	2,182	1,725
1963	20,134	8,527	6,003	3,774	1,830
1964[r]	20,594	8,911	5,242	4,720	1,721
1965[r]	20,670	9,747	3,626	5,329	1,968
1966[p]	24,229	11,951	4,052	5,903	2,323
1967[E]	26,200	13,600	4,400	5,700	2,500

Note: Includes military and nonmilitary sales and research, development, test and evaluation. Because of changes in source material, individual years are not always strictly comparable.

[r] Revised. Nonaerospace figures exclude nonaerospace establishments owned and operated by aerospace companies.

[p] Preliminary.

[E] Estimate.

Source: Aerospace Industries Association.

Again because of the disproportionately lower educational attainment of Negroes, their opportunities of employment in production work are greater than in salaried employment. The high precision job shop nature of missile work and its heavy engineering and research content require skills and technical knowledge which greatly limit opportunities for those lacking in education or experience.

In 1967, the product mix of aerospace showed the full impact of

FIGURE 3. *Changing Pattern of Aerospace Sales*

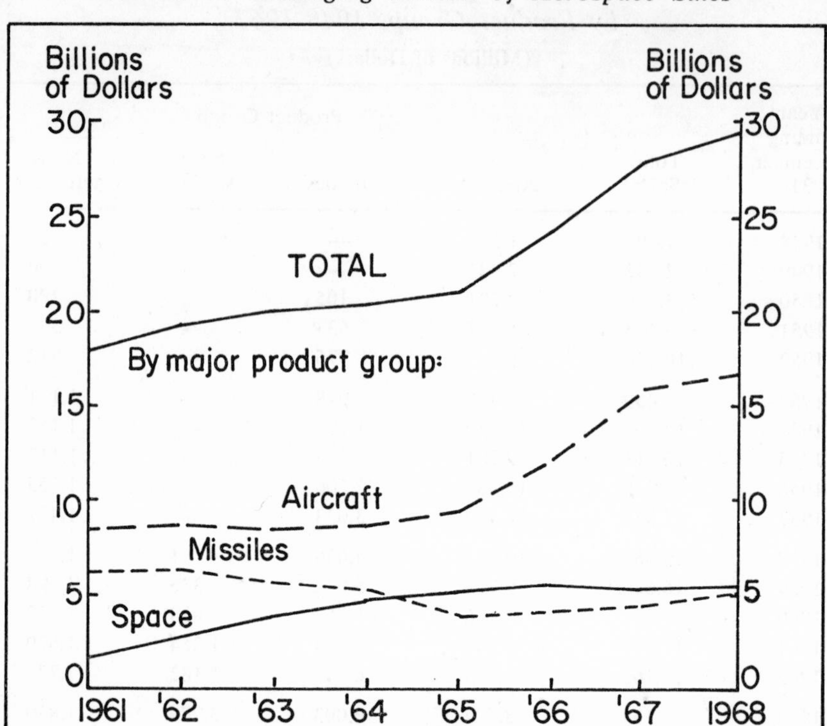

Source: Aerospace Industries Association for data and estimates. Chart by National Industrial Conference Board.

the Vietnam war and the boom in commercial aviation. Figure 3 reflects the leveling off of the space program, a slight increase in missiles, and a decided increase in aircraft sales; the latter results from a 52 percent increase in Defense Department procurement of aircraft, including helicopters, between 1965 and 1967, and an increase in commercial airplane sales of more than 100 percent in the same period, with the trend expected to continue in 1968. The outlook for Negro employment is enhanced by these developments since they involve a trend toward mass production and consequent relatively greater need of semiskilled labor for which the inexperienced and disadvantaged can be more easily trained and utilized.

OCCUPATIONAL DISTRIBUTION

We have already noted that the aerospace industry utilizes a high percentage of salaried and professional employees relative to total

TABLE 8. *Occupational Distribution of Employees Five Aerospace Companies, 1966*

Occupation	Total Number	Total Percent	Company A	Company B	Company C	Company D	Company E
Officials and managers	30,150	9.1	6,676	15,823	6,087	684	880
Professionals	68,797	20.8	28,440	20,902	14,054	4,280	1,121
Technicians	26,992	8.2	5,012	16,549	4,488	554	389
Sales workers	195	0.1	169	—	13	—	13
Office and clerical	52,872	16.0	13,571	27,699	8,158	1,564	1,880
Craftsmen (Skilled)	70,418	21.3	22,063	31,248	12,838	977	3,292
Operatives (Semiskilled)	71,957	21.7	12,477	25,371	30,481	991	2,637
Laborers (Unskilled)	4,301	1.3	461	328	3,397	1	114
Service workers	4,922	1.5	1,130	1,690	1,710	150	242
Total	330,604	100.0	89,999	139,610	81,226	9,201	10,568

Source: Data in author's possession.

employment. Table 8 gives the broad occupational grouping for five key representative companies. In Companies A, B, and D, and for the five companies as a group, the number of salaried workers exceeds that of hourly; in both A and D, the professional group is the largest single category and in C it is the second largest. In Company D, which is primarily a missile research and development and manufacturing operation, the professional group is by far the most significant one. This preponderance of salaried personnel exists despite the absence of large sales staffs. Selling to the government is a managerial, technical, or professional job.

Among the production workers, craftsmen is the largest occupational group in two of the five companies, and in Company B the largest in the entire work force. The high precision content of the work, its job shop characteristics and the lack of repetitive operations in many of the work situations, and above all the absolute need for high quality and zero defects in workmanship in order to assure human safety, all increase the demand for skilled craftsmen rather than semiskilled operatives or unskilled laborers. Indeed the five companies had a total of only 4,301 laborers, 3,397 in one company. The three lowest classifications were only 24.5 percent of the total number of employees. In contrast, more than one-half of all employees of the Big Three automobile companies—General Motors, Ford, and Chrysler—are classified as operatives. In automobiles,

TABLE 9. *Occupational Distribution of Employees, 21 Companies, 127 Establishments in the Aerospace Industry, 1966*

Occupation	Number of Employees	Percent of Total
Officials and managers	71,328	9.1
Professionals	179,436	22.8
Technicians	63,999	8.1
Sales workers	720	0.1
Office and clerical	130,261	16.5
Craftsmen (Skilled)	164,991	20.9
Operatives (Semiskilled)	155,167	19.7
Laborers (Unskilled)	8,065	1.0
Service workers	14,055	1.8
Total	788,022	100.0

Source: Data in author's possession.

operatives, laborers, and service workers comprise nearly two-thirds of the work force.

The occupational distribution for the industry is further explored in Table 9, which contains data covering 21 companies employing 788,022 employees in 127 establishments. This represents about two-thirds of the total labor force in the aerospace industry.

The data in Table 9 show that professionals are the largest occupational group with craftsmen second, and operatives third. Salaried employees, including office and clerical, are a clear majority of the labor force in this large sample, with the employees who are semiskilled (operatives) and unskilled (laborers and service workers) accounting for less than 25 percent of the total.

The significance of the aerospace industry's occupational distribution for Negroes is, again, that Negroes are concentrated in those classifications for which the industry has the least demand; and Negroes are most underrepresented in jobs for which the industry has the most pressing needs.

EARNINGS AND UNIONIZATION

The aerospace industry, with its emphasis on high skills, is a well-paying industry. In 1966, for example, production employees in "aircraft and parts" averaged $143.32 per week and $3.31 per hour. This placed them slightly below such industries as "motor vehicles and equipment" and "blast furnaces and basic steel products," but substantially above the 1966 average for manufacturing ($112.34 per week and $2.72 per hour), or durable goods manufacturing ($122.09 per week and $2.90 per hour).[5]

The aerospace industry generally pays the same wage rates regardless of location. In the lower wage areas, this places workers in the industry close to the top of the industrial scale. Benefits are also usually paid on a national basis, with widespread acceptance of generous pension, health and welfare, and other fringes provided at employer expense.

Most aerospace plants are unionized, with the International Association of Machinists and Aerospace Workers having the largest number of employees under contract, and the United Automobile, Aerospace and Agricultural Implement Workers (UAW) a close second. Both unions added "Aerospace" to their names after being founded by workers in other industries. In addition, a large number of craft unions, organizations of guards, and even unions of professional and technical employees have contracts with aerospace companies. Unionization occurred for the most part during the World War II period. A few companies—Northrop in Southern California, Grumman on Long Island, New York, and General Electric's missile and space operations in the Philadelphia area—are nonunion, and some plants are unionized by other than the IAM or UAW. Union racial policies will be analyzed in ensuing sections of the study in so far as they bear on company policies.

INDUSTRIAL LOCATION

Plants of the aerospace industry are located in all parts of the country, but Southern California has by far the heaviest concentration of the industry. As of October 1966, the data in Table 10 show that three Southern California labor market areas accounted for 24.4 percent of the employment in the industry. A total of 34.5 percent of the industry's employment is found in major West Coast centers, with Seattle, home of Boeing, having the second largest concentration of workers.

No area outside the West Coast could boast more than 3.9 percent of the industry's employment, but twelve areas had over half the industry's workers. In most cities outside of Southern California,

5. Data from U. S. Bureau of Labor Statistics.

TABLE 10. *Employment in the Twelve Largest Aerospace Labor Market Areas, 1966*

	Aerospace Employment (thousands)	Percent of Total U. S. Aerospace Employment
Total U. S. aerospace employment	1,322.1	100.0
Total Twelve largest labor market areas	749.2	56.7
Total West Coast labor market areas	456.3	34.5
Total Major Southern California labor market areas	323.2	24.4
Los Angeles, Long Beach, California	240.2	18.2
Seattle, Washington	98.0	7.4
Anaheim, Santa Ana, Garden Grove, California	52.5	4.0
New York, New York	51.3	3.9
Hartford, Connecticut	46.5	3.5
Philadelphia, Pennsylvania	45.8	3.5
St. Louis, Missouri	41.5	3.1
Dallas-Fort Worth, Texas	40.0	3.0
San Jose, California	35.1	2.7
Wichita, Kansas	34.4	2.6
Boston, Massachusetts	33.4	2.5
San Diego, California	30.5	2.3

Note: The Atlanta, Ga. labor market has almost as many aerospace employees as has San Diego.

Source: Aerospace Industries Association and data in author's possession.

one aerospace company accounts for most of the employment: Boeing in Seattle, Lockheed in Atlanta, United Aircraft in Hartford, and McDonnell in St. Louis. Employment in the industry in such an area is thus almost completely dependent upon the ability of one company to maintain its sales position. In aerospace, this, of course, usually means success in obtaining and holding the employment-generating government contracts.

Superficially, the location of the industry would seem advantageous to Negro employment, for, despite the heavy West Coast concentration, the industry is found in many areas in which Negroes are a significant portion of the total population. As we shall note later in the study, however, testing and product requirements lead most aerospace companies to locate away from center city and thus away from the Negro population concentrations. This aggravates the Negro's search for work problems and is a factor in the low percentage of Negroes in the industry.

CHAPTER III.

World War II
From Exclusion to Utilization

The pioneer manufacturers of flying machines sought to accomplish their tasks with the aid of an almost wholly white labor force. As a fledgling industry with modest labor requirements during World War I, the aircraft manufacturers, unlike their counterparts in automobiles or steel, were not required to import southern Negro labor to keep their factories manned. Moreover, the manufacture of planes, aircraft engines, and components remained, up to World War II, largely on a job basis. The product sales volume did not justify elaborate work division or mass production techniques. Hence there was little demand for unskilled labor, and in the 1920's and 1930's, very few Negroes had the training or skill to work as aircraft mechanics. In 1940, for example, only 186 nonwhite employees, 0.2 percent of the labor force, were found in the "aircraft and parts" industry by the census of that year. (See Table 11.) The few Negroes in the industry were nearly all janitors, porters, or outside laborers.

The virtual exclusion of Negroes from the aircraft industry prior to World War II was certainly consistent with conscious owner-managerial policies. *Fortune* magazine reported in the spring of 1940 that the aircraft industry had "an almost universal prejudice against Negroes . . . you almost never see Negroes in aircraft factories . . . there is little concealment about the anti-Negro policy. . . ."[6]

Company presidents both before and immediately after the Japanese attack on Pearl Harbor, were very frank indeed about the industry's racial policies. The president of Vultee (now a division of General Dynamics) told a Negro organization that "it is not the policy of this company to employ people other than of the Caucasian race. . . ."[7] When plans were announced by North American Aviation,

6. *Fortune,* "Half a Million Workers," XXIII (March 1943), pp. 98, 163.
7. *Ibid.*

TABLE 11. *Total Employed Persons by Race and Sex Aircraft and Parts Manufacturing Industry,*[a] *1940-1960*

Year	All Employees			Male			Female		
	Total	Nonwhite	Percent Nonwhite	Total	Nonwhite	Percent Nonwhite	Total	Nonwhite	Percent Nonwhite
1940	107,131	186	0.2	102,526	182	0.2	4,605	4	0.1
1950	257,310	4,230	1.6	224,310	4,050	1.8	33,000	180	0.5
1960	644,390	23,480	3.6	541,680	20,588	3.8	102,710	2,892	2.8

[a] SIC, 372; Census, 268.

Source: *U. S. Census of Population:*
1940: Vol. III, *The Labor Force,* Table 76.
1950: P-E No. 1D, *Industrial Characteristics,* Table 2.
1960: PC (2) 7F, *Industrial Characteristics,* Table 3.

Inc., to build a major bomber plant near Kansas City, Kansas, in March 1941, a group of Negro civic leaders inquired about the prospects for employment of members of their race. The president of the Company was quoted as follows:

> "We will receive applications from both white and Negro workers. However, the Negroes will be considered only as janitors and in other similar capacities. . . .
>
> "While we are in complete sympathy with the Negro, it is against the company policy to employ them as mechanics or aircraft workers.
>
> "We use none except white workers in the plant . . . at Inglewood [Cal.] and the plant in Dallas and we intend to maintain the same policy in Kansas City. . . ."[8]

Likewise, Glenn L. Martin, founder of the Baltimore company of the same name, told a Congressional committee in March 1942, that segregation practices in the state, plus fear of walkouts by white workers who would object to Negro employment, made it impractical to employ Negroes.[9] And a recruiter of the Boeing Company told a Negro applicant that there was "no place for Negro workers. . . ."[10]

There were some exceptions to the industry's initial negative approach to Negro employment. Lockheed in Southern California recruited Negro employees in the early forties without waiting for government prodding, as did United Aircraft in New England, and Bell in Buffalo, New York.[11] Moreover, companies like North American, Boeing, and Martin completely altered their policies in the face of all-out war, the need to utilize all available manpower, government pressure, and obvious morality and decency. The labor force in "aircraft and parts" rose to a high of 1,345,600 in 1943. Plants and companies which had lily-white labor complements before the war, trained and took on Negroes in a variety of jobs. The same North American president who said Negroes could work only as janitors at the Kansas City plant, was pictured talking to skilled Negro metal workers one year later by the Negro newspaper which quoted his early statement.[12] Negroes made up about 5 percent

8. *The Call,* Kansas City, March 21, 1941.
9. *Norfolk Journal & Guide,* January 10, 1942.
10. Associated Negro Press report, *Louisiana Weekly,* December 13, 1941.
11. The information herein is based on the author's field notes of this period. See also, Herbert R. Northrup, *Organized Labor and the Negro* (New York: Harper & Brothers, 1944), pp. 205-209.
12. *The Call,* Kansas City, March 20 and April 10, 1942.

of this plant's 17,000 workers and were found in nearly all blue collar departments and occupations.

In most northern plants, Negroes thus not only gained entrance to the industry, but also to skilled production jobs. In the South progress was much slower. New plants built in Texas, Louisiana, Georgia, and even in border areas like St. Louis hired few Negroes and operated with segregated facilities. The Fairchild Aircraft Company established an all-Negro plant at its Hagerstown, Maryland, works. The Douglas plant at Tulsa, Oklahoma, however, did employ a large number of Negroes without such segregation. On the other hand, the Vultee plant at Nashville, Tennessee, added few Negroes, even after a directive to do so by the President's Committee on Fair Employment Practice.

Negro women also were introduced into aircraft factories for the first time during the war. This was primarily in the North, although in St. Louis and the Cincinnati areas, where segregation was still practiced, Negro women were also employed.

There were a great many obstacles which thwarted Negroes, who wanted aircraft jobs in this period. Their lack of training has already been noted. In many areas, including but not confined to the South, Negro groups had to apply great pressure to gain entrance to training opportunities, including those which were taxpayer financed. Sometimes, the training for Negroes was segregated, and inferior. In many cases, valuable time and jobs were lost because of the procrastination in making training available to Negroes. In other cases, training for Negroes omitted preparation for certain key jobs.

Plant location was also a bar to Negro employment. Huge new plants had to be constructed in outlying areas. Public transportation was often poorest from Negro neighborhoods and since fewer Negroes had automobiles, car pools were more difficult to arrange.

On the other hand, the existence of aircraft and other war industries drew Negroes, as well as whites, to new areas. Farm-city migration was accelerated. Negro communities grew up or were greatly enlarged in the West Coast cities of San Diego, Seattle, and especially Oakland and Los Angeles. The labor force of these areas, as well as of the industry, was changed dramatically.

Union policies played a minor role in racial policies of the aircraft industry during World War II, although many of the plants became unionized by either the International Association of Machinists or the United Automobile Workers. At this time, the IAM had a provision in its initiation ritual which pledged members to recommend membership only to "qualified white mechanics." This provision was ignored by some of its locals, particularly the one at Lockheed's southern California operations. In some cases, IAM officials or local unions strongly opposed Negro employment. Generally, however, since few of its aircraft contracts then provided for the union shop, it did not take a position on Negro employment, although certainly at best, this union then was no supporter of fair employment practice, and in some cases supported or institutionalized the opposition of white workers to upgrading or employment of Negroes.

The UAW had an avowed equalitarian policy which in one case led it to fire an organizer who called a strike against Negro upgrading in a Curtiss-Wright plant, and to order the men back to work.[13] The UAW also actively solicited Negro members. It too, however, had few union shop agreements and left hiring and upgrading policies largely to management, within the general framework of the collective agreements of that period.

Negroes' greatest gains in the aircraft industry occurred in the automotive plants which were converted to war production. Here the Negro was no stranger, and here there would be jobs when the war was over. In the aircraft industry proper, Negro employment at the peak probably did not exceed 50,000—somewhat less than 4 percent of the industry's employment.[14]

From a peak of 1,345,600 in 1943, employment in aircraft and parts declined to 788,100 in 1945 and to 237,300 in 1946.[15] Most Negro employees were laid off with the mass of white workers who lost their jobs as plants closed at the end of the war. But not all gains disappeared. Those Negroes who were trained were better capable of finding new jobs. And the lily-white caste of the industry was forever ended, although in varying degrees among different companies. The 1950 decennial census found 4,230 Negroes in the aircraft and parts industry—1.6 percent of those employed (see Table 11).

13. *New York Times,* December 3, 1943.
14. See Northrup, *Organized Labor and the Negro, loc. cit.*
15. Data from U. S. Bureau of Labor Statistics.

CHAPTER IV.

From Aircraft to Aerospace, 1945-1960

The aircraft industry regrouped and recovered very slowly after the great cutbacks which followed the end of World War II hostilities. Single companies, at the receipt of telegrams from the Pentagon, laid workers off 10,000 or even 50,000 at a time. Whole huge plants were abandoned in locations throughout the country. Demands for civilian aircraft revived, but required only a small fraction of the wartime factory or worker demands, and the government was very slow to develop a significant interest in missile and space vehicles despite their demonstrated effectiveness by Germany. Employment in the industry remained fairly constant at about 250,000 until the outbreak of the Korean War.

NEGRO EMPLOYMENT, 1945-1950

Negro employees were hard hit by the postwar layoffs. As a newly hired group, they had little seniority. Many new plants where they had made impressive gains were completely shut down: Curtiss-Wright in St. Louis and Cincinnati (Evendale), Douglas at Tulsa, and North American at Kansas City, are examples. In addition, a number of companies, such as Northrop and Lockheed, shut down facilities in heavily populated areas of Los Angeles and moved their remaining operations to plants located in suburban or outlying areas. Such moves were motivated by sound business considerations, because of the need for space for testing products and the obvious dangers caused by aircraft maneuvering in populated areas. Nevertheless, the impact on Negroes was severe, because it left plants concentrated in areas where Negroes could not obtain housing.

The location of the major plants of the industry posed even greater obstacles for Negro workers as the post-World War II years passed because of the increasing substitution of private automobile transportation for the public urban systems. This has tended to increase Negro isolation in center cities and restrict their search for work: people need jobs to buy automobiles, but need automobiles to reach jobs. Negroes are disproportionately caught in this circle, as a result of discrimination in housing and in credit opportunities, their concentration in the cities, and their relative lack of education and knowledge of the labor market.[16]

There were also a few positive factors which contributed to Negro employment in the postwar era. Facilities abandoned by one company were taken over by others after some period, and in a number of cases without some of the less favorable characteristics for Negroes which had featured wartime operations. For example, although Curtiss-Wright was a significant employer of Negroes during the war, it did conform to segregation practices where they existed. In late 1945, McDonnell Aircraft Corporation took over the abandoned facility at Lambert Field, St. Louis. McDonnell's first act after acquiring the plant, " . . . prior to moving its personnel into the buildings, was to desegregate rest rooms, dressing rooms, locker areas, drinking fountains, rest areas and cafeterias."[17] In so doing, McDonnell followed a policy inaugurated in 1943, when it acquired a former garage in downtown St. Louis as its first major plant. Despite the fact that St. Louis was then a segregated city, this plant was operated without segregation. About 3 percent of McDonnell's employees were then colored.[18]

Other facilities which were desegregated when put back in operation by new owners or operators were the former Curtiss-Wright plant at Evandale, a Cincinnati, Ohio, suburb, which General Electric converted into a major jet engine facility; the former North American plant in Grand Prairie, near Dallas, Texas, which was reactivated by Chance-Vought, then a division of United Aircraft, but now of Ling-Temco-Vought; and the former Bell Aircraft complex at Marietta, near Atlanta, Georgia, which Lockheed now operates. These

16. On these problems see, in general, *The Negroes in the United States: Their Economic and Social Situation,* Bulletin No. 1511, U. S. Bureau of Labor Statistics, Washington, 1966; *Social and Economic Conditions in the United States,* U. S. Bureau of Labor Statistics Report No. 332 and U. S. Bureau of the Census, Current Population Reports, Series P-23, No. 24, 1967; Karl E. and Alma F. Tauber, *Negroes in Cities* (Chicago: Aldine Publishing Company, 1965); and especially J. R. Meyer, J. F. Kain, and M. Wohl, *The Urban Transportation Problem* (Cambridge, Mass.: Harvard University Press, 1965), pp. 144-170.
17. R. C. Krone, "The Civil Rights Act and its Effect in Missouri," address before the 64th Annual Conference, Missouri Association for Social Welfare, October 29, 1964. Mr. Krone is Vice-President—Personnel, McDonnell Aircraft Corporation.
18. *Ibid.*

three facilities were not reactivated until the Korean War period. Both General Electric and Chance-Vought immediately desegregated their plants, but Lockheed followed local practices for a time before doing so.[19] Neither Chance-Vought, nor later Bell Helicopter, which opened new facilities near Fort Worth in the early 1950's, employed Negroes to any degree in other than menial jobs during this period.

Despite some favorable aspects, the period 1945-1950 was hardly one of progress for Negro employment in the aircraft industry. By 1950, the decennial census found that only 1.6 percent of the approximately 250,000 persons employed in the industry were Negroes. (See Table 11.) To be sure, this was a far better showing than reported by the 1940 census. In the interim, however, the percentage of Negro employment in the industry had risen to 3 or 4 percent of the industry's labor force at the peak of wartime employment, and then declined by 50 percent as a result of the postwar layoffs.

THE KOREAN WAR TO 1960

The demands of the Korean War pushed up employment substantially in the aircraft industry and the commitment of the United States thereafter to maintain air supremacy kept employment on an upward trend until 1958. From the post-World War II level of approximately 250,000, employment in the aircraft and parts industry rose to 467,800 in 1951, 795,500 in 1953, and peaked at 895,800 in 1957.[20] As already noted, huge plants which were abandoned in 1944 and 1945 were reopened, and new facilities built. Vast sums were committed to research and development as manned aircraft entered the turbojet age, and new metals, electronic controls, and technology were needed to handle the new speeds, distances, and heights which could be flown.

The Korean War boom helped to generate the lowest unemployment level in the post-World War II era. Negroes profited, as they have in boom times, by gaining a share of the work opportunities in war industries. Severe cutbacks, however, occurred from 1958 to 1961 and employment in the aircraft and parts industry fell to 619,200 in the latter year. One must presume that large numbers

19. On Lockheed's policy, see E. G. Mattison, "Integrating the Work Force in Southern Industry," in Herbert R. Northrup and Richard L. Rowan (eds.), *The Negro and Employment Opportunity* (Ann Arbor, Mich.: Bureau of Industrial Relations, University of Michigan, 1965), pp. 147-154.

20. Data from Aerospace Industries Association, based upon U. S. Bureau of Labor Statistics figures.

TABLE 12. *Total Employed Persons, Aircraft and Parts Manufacturing Industry Occupational Distribution by Race and Sex, 1960*

Occupation	All Employees			Male			Female		
	Total	Nonwhite	Percent Nonwhite	Total	Nonwhite	Percent Nonwhite	Total	Nonwhite	Percent Nonwhite
Managers, officials, and proprietors	19,215	22	0.1	18,238	22	0.1	977	—	—
Professional, technical, and kindred workers	143,933	2,816	2.0	137,560	2,715	2.0	6,373	101	1.6
Clerical and kindred workers	108,742	1,501	1.4	48,370	1,030	2.1	60,372	471	0.8
Sales workers	3,030	—	—	2,971	—	—	59	—	—
Craftsmen, foremen, and kindred workers	167,173	4,338	2.6	162,775	4,217	2.6	4,398	121	2.8
Operatives and kindred workers	175,461	10,731	6.1	148,193	8,993	6.1	27,268	1,738	6.4
Laborers	5,219	981	18.8	5,038	961	19.1	181	20	11.0
Service workers	10,855	2,395	22.1	9,314	2,055	22.1	1,541	340	22.1
Occupation not reported	10,762	675	6.3	9,221	574	6.2	1,541	101	6.6
Total	644,390	23,459	3.6	541,680	20,567	3.8	102,710	2,892	2.8

Source: *U. S. Census of Population 1960*, PC(2) 7A, *Occupational Characteristics*, Table 36.

TABLE 13. *Total Employed Persons, Aircraft and Parts Manufacturing Industry for Selected States, by Race, 1940-1960*

State	1960			1950			1940		
	All Employees	Negroes	Percent Negro	All Employees	Negroes	Percent Negro	All Employees	Negroes	Percent Negro
California	182,826	6,665	3.6	82,534	1,301	1.6	37,719	10	*
Connecticut	57,743	782	1.4	18,234	120	0.7	10,817	3	*
Washington	54,118	1,034	1.9	17,254	155	0.9	5,449	—	—
New York	51,415	1,681	3.3	26,513	378	1.4	13,791	18	0.1
Ohio	49,500	2,023	4.1	16,078	682	4.2	4,299	14	0.3
Texas	40,178	838	2.1	23,116	339	1.5	118	4	3.4
Kansas	32,141	547	1.7	12,960	104	0.8	1,582	—	—
Missouri	22,841	861	3.8	5,979	104	1.7	806	8	1.0
New Jersey	22,452	523	2.3	15,762	211	1.3	10,993	11	0.1
Indiana	21,425	477	2.2	9,545	209	2.2	2,835	7	0.2
Georgia	12,973	814	6.3	66	7	10.6	11	—	—
Pennsylvania	11,921	158	1.3	4,917	61	1.2	3,773	19	0.5
Massachusetts	11,252	110	1.0	2,540	8	0.3	—	—	—
Oklahoma	6,346	108	1.7	818	24	2.9	137	—	—
Florida	3,833	107	2.8	209	5	2.4	54	—	—

* Less than 0.05 percent.

Sources: U. S. *Census of Population:*
1940: Vol. III, *The Labor Force,* parts 2-5, Table 18.
1950: Vol. II, *Characteristics of the Population,* State volumes, Table 83.
1960: PC(1)D, *Detailed Characteristics,* State volumes, Table 129.

of Negro aircraft workers became unemployed as a result of these declines. Yet over the decade, as the data in Table 11 show, nonwhite employment (which is overwhelmingly Negro) rose from 1.6 percent to 3.6 percent of the total "aircraft and parts" work force.

The skill distribution shown by the 1960 census reveals the usual heavy concentration in the unskilled and semiskilled jobs and the under-representation of nonwhites in the higher classifications[21] (Table 12). Thus in 1960, 22.1 percent of the service workers, 18.8 percent of the laborers, and 6.1 percent of the operatives in the aircraft and parts industry were nonwhite; but beyond that, nonwhite participation varied from 2.6 percent of the craftsmen and foremen to no sales personnel and virtually no managers. Most sales personnel, as already noted, selling to the government are classified as professional or managerial by the companies. Few if any Negroes were in such jobs in 1960, but recruitment of some Negro engineers and technicians for inside work was not by then novel.

The aircraft industry in 1960 was more advanced than many others in the utilization of nonwhite women, both in the factory and in the office. As in the case of men, the largest number of nonwhite women in blue collar jobs were classified as semiskilled operatives; in the offices, nonwhite women held various clerical jobs. Negro female employment in aircraft plants was most common around 1960 in Southern California, and least common (as it is today) in the South.

Tables 13 and 14 explore Negro employment in the aircraft and parts industries on state and regional bases for the principal areas of aircraft production. Negro employment by state in 1960 was highest in Georgia, a temporary phenomenon that did not last after the major plant in the state greatly expanded production in the more skilled areas. Southern California, Ohio, New York, and Missouri were the leading areas in the percentage of Negro employment at this time, and New York and California showed the greatest gains over the two decades. The substantial improvement of Negro representation in the industry in the two decades reported in Table 13 occurred throughout the country. Yet in no state with substantial employment in the industry did the proportion of Negroes exceed 4.2 percent.

---

21. These data include nonwhites other than Negroes. This causes a slight distortion for Southern California data, where a number of Orientals are employed, but even there the numbers of nonwhite, non-Negroes are small.

TABLE 14. *Total Employed Persons Aircraft and Parts Manufacturing Industry for Seven Standard Metropolitan Statistical Areas, by Race 1950 and 1960*

Standard Metropolitan Statistical Area	1960 All Employees	1960 Negro	1960 Percent Negro	1950 All Employees	1950 Negro	1950 Percent Negro
Los Angeles-Long Beach	153,337	6,283	4.1	70,209	1,183	1.7
Seattle, Washington	50,276	967	1.9	16,274	152	0.9
New York	37,826	1,558	4.1	19,643	358	1.8
Wichita, Kansas	26,254	520	2.0	11,681	97	0.8
Fort Worth, Texas	22,690	342	1.5	15,028	237	1.6
St. Louis, Mo.-Ill.	20,366	874	4.3	5,165	103	2.0
Philadelphia, Pa.-N.J.	4,221	136	3.2	2,366	67	2.8

Source: *U. S. Census of Population:*
1950: Vol. II, *Characteristics of the Population,* State volumes, Table 83.
1960: PC(1)D, *Detailed Characteristics,* State volumes, Table 129.

Table 14 provides the same data for seven Standard Metropolitan Statistical Areas—that is, cities and suburbs comprising overall labor markets. These were in 1960 among the largest centers of aircraft and parts production. The superior position of Negroes in the Los Angeles, New York, and St. Louis areas and the relatively poor showing in Fort Worth and Seattle are emphasized by these data. When, however, one compares the employment data in Table 14 with 1960 population statistics, it was apparent that Negroes in the Los Angeles SMSA had the greatest opportunities for jobs in aircraft plants and those in Fort Worth, the least. Fort Worth with a city population that was about 16 percent Negro in 1960 had no higher a percentage of Negro aircraft employment than did Seattle, the population of which was 5 percent Negro. St. Louis had twice the proportion of Negro population as did New York and Los Angeles, but all three had about the same proportion of Negro aircraft workers. Yet no other area had more than a 4.3 percent proportion of Negro aircraft employees.

NIXON COMMITTEE FINDINGS

The extent and character of progress made by Negroes in the aircraft industry during the 1950's is corroborated by studies made for the President's Committee on Government Contracts from 1957 to 1960. Known as the Nixon Committee, because it was chaired

TABLE 15. *Aerospace Industry, Total and Negro Employment by Major Occupational Groups, 13 Companies, 17 Plants, 1959*

Occupational Groups	All Employees	Negro	Percent Negro
Professional and technical	42,274	187	0.4
Supervisory	14,774	44	0.3
Clerical and stenographic	26,458	329	1.2
Skilled	63,443	2,301	3.6
Semiskilled	33,699	2,450	7.3
Unskilled	11,901	1,037	8.7
Other	5,099	188	3.7
Total	197,648	6,536	3.3

Source: President's Committee on Government Contracts (Nixon Committee) files.

by the then Vice-President, this Committee was charged with discouraging discrimination by government contractors. Data gathered by it relating to seventeen plants of thirteen aerospace companies for 1959 are summarized in Table 15. These data show about the same over all percentage of Negro employment as do the census data, and the same concentration of Negroes in lower rated jobs.

The data in Table 15 are primarily for aircraft and aircraft parts manufacturing enterprises, rather than for missile and space production. This accounts for the relatively heavy concentration of semi-skilled and unskilled jobs and the relatively small number of professional and other salaried groups. As missile and space vehicle production increased and aircraft production declined in the early 1960's, Negro employment was initially adversely affected.

DEVELOPMENTS IN THE SOUTH

By 1960, the major aircraft companies in the Dallas-Fort Worth area had made little progress in employing and upgrading Negroes. In fact, very few Negroes were employed in these plants except in laboring and service jobs. Moreover, the facilities of at least two of the major plants there remained segregated. Progress toward elimination of segregation and toward upgrading of Negro personnel had been started under the prodding of The Nixon Committee. Before, however, any real progress could be made, employment in Southwest aerospace plants suffered sharp declines. General Dynamics dropped from 27,000 in 1956 to 6,000 in 1960 and Chance-Vought from

16,800 in 1957 to 7,253 in 1960. Bell Helicopter remained at about 2,500. The lack of progress in Negro employment in the 1950's and the slow revival during the next decade were to have profoundly adverse effects on Negro employment in the area in the 1960's.

The principal plant in the Southeast aerospace industry is the huge facility at Marietta, Georgia, near Atlanta, which was built during World War II, and taken over and expanded by Lockheed during the Korean War. Lockheed hired substantially more Negroes than did the Southwest plants, but it too operated on a segregated basis in this period. Negroes were used on production lines, which were segregated, but the company resisted demands of the local affiliate of the International Association of Machinists to establish a segregated seniority system. When layoffs occurred in the late 1950's, white workers were faced with a choice of integrating the seniority lines or suffering further layoffs. In this way, Lockheed moved toward integration and then to the affirmative action which has figured so prominently in the leadership of the Southeast in aerospace employment in the 1960's that is described in the next chapter.

CHAPTER V.

Employment Expansion and Affirmative Action, 1960-1966

The 1960's did not commence auspiciously for Negro employment in the aerospace industry. The decline in employment in the aircraft industry which began in 1957 continued through 1964. Missile and space vehicle employment rose to offset or nearly offset that decline, but the character of the work in the two main segments of aerospace is quite different.

Missile and space vehicle work is, as has been noted, essentially of a job shop character, with much greater proportionate need for skilled craftsmen, technicians, and professionals than aircraft. Given the relative scarcity of Negroes with these skills, it was not till late 1963 and 1964, when civilian aircraft production, military procurement, and the space program all boomed in concert with increased emphasis on civil rights, that Negro employment in the aerospace industry began to show both qualitative and quantitative advances over the late 1950's.

THE EARLY MISSILE AND SPACE PERIOD, 1960-1964

Table 16 shows employment in 21 aerospace companies and 140 plants by race and sex for the total country and for various regions, based on data collected by the Plans for Progress organization. These data, of course, are not strictly comparable to those collected either by the Bureau of the Census or by the Nixon Committee. They do demonstrate, however, that Negro employment did not gain in the 1960-1963 period and probably even declined. The principal reason appears to be the changing product mix from aircraft to missiles and space vehicles, which offset company "affirmative action" programs, joint industry-government activities, such as the Plans for Progress program, and government pressure exerted through procurement policies designed to expand Negro employment.

TABLE 16. *Aerospace Industry Employment by Race, Sex, and Region*
21 Companies, 140 Establishments, 1963

Region	All Employees			Male			Female		
	Total	Negro	Percent Negro	Total	Negro	Percent Negro	Total	Negro	Percent Negro
Northeast	147,395	3,598	2.4	128,764	3,258	2.5	18,631	340	1.8
New England	69,823	1,048	1.5	60,094	975	1.6	9,729	73	0.8
Middle Atlantic	77,572	2,550	3.3	68,670	2,283	3.3	8,902	267	3.0
South	60,175	1,095	1.8	52,152	945	1.8	8,023	150	1.9
Southeast	29,314	506	1.7	25,224	394	1.6	4,090	112	2.7
Southwest	30,861	589	1.9	26,928	551	2.0	3,933	38	1.0
Midwest	87,858	3,310	3.8	77,566	3,015	3.9	10,292	295	2.9
West Coast	352,547	10,284	2.9	284,025	8,293	2.9	68,522	1,991	2.9
Southern California	234,144	8,303	3.5	184,679	6,660	3.6	49,465	1,643	3.3
Other West Coast	118,403	1,981	1.7	99,346	1,633	1.6	19,057	348	1.8
Total United States	647,975	18,287	2.8	542,507	15,511	2.9	105,468	2,776	2.6

Source: Data supplied to Plans for Progress.

Note: Geographic definitions are as follows:

New England: Maine, Vermont, New Hampshire, Massachusetts, Connecticut, and Rhode Island.
Middle Atlantic: New York, Pennsylvania, New Jersey, Maryland, and Delaware.
Southeast: Virginia, West Virginia, North Carolina, South Carolina, Georgia, Florida, Alabama, Mississippi, Louisiana, Tennessee, and Kentucky.
Southwest: Texas, Oklahoma, New Mexico, and Arizona.
West Coast: Washington, Oregon, California, Idaho, and Nevada.
Midwest: All Midwest and Rocky Mountain States. Actual plants only in Colorado and Midwest except for small military installations.

In addition, employment in the South continued to lag and meaningful integration had not gone far by then.

In 1963, *Business Week* magazine made a study of what this changed product mix meant to the labor force requirements at Douglas Aircraft Company. Figure 4 summarizes these changes. The *Business Week* survey found that the hourly worker was not only declining in importance in aerospace, "but where he survives . . . [is] both more skilled and more versatile. The rigid tolerances and quality control

FIGURE 4. *How Douglas' Labor Needs Have Changed*

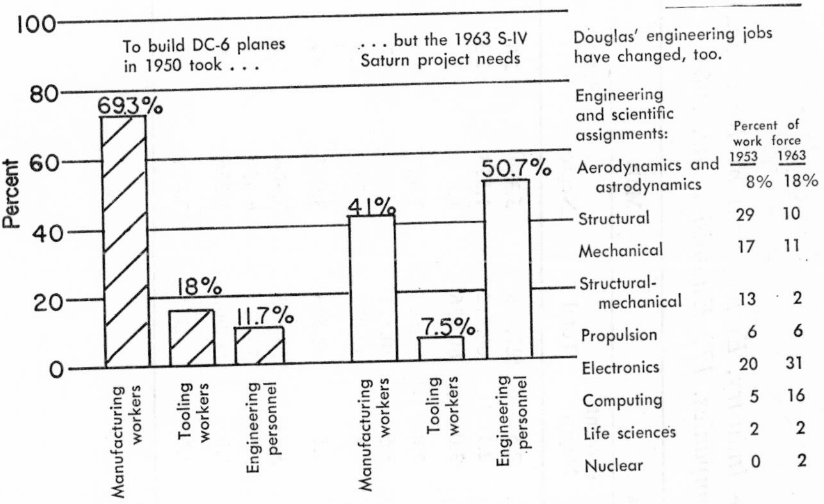

To build DC-6 planes in 1950 took . . .

	Percent
Manufacturing workers	69.3%
Tooling workers	18%
Engineering personnel	11.7%

. . . but the 1963 S-IV Saturn project needs

	Percent
Manufacturing workers	41%
Tooling workers	7.5%
Engineering personnel	50.7%

Douglas' engineering jobs have changed, too.

Engineering and scientific assignments:	Percent of work force 1953	1963
Aerodynamics and astrodynamics	8%	18%
Structural	29	10
Mechanical	17	11
Structural-mechanical	13	2
Propulsion	6	6
Electronics	20	31
Computing	5	16
Life sciences	2	2
Nuclear	0	2

Source: *Business Week,* June 22, 1963, by permission of McGraw-Hill Company.

requirements of spacecraft demand the first characteristic, its 'custom-made' nature the second. . . ."[22] The changing product mix of the industry during this period drastically reduced demands for such lower skilled jobs as riveters, assemblers, fabricators, and foundry workers and greatly increased jobs for engineers and electronic technicians.[23]

In all the areas of job increase, proportionately fewer Negroes had the background even to qualify them for training. The results, of course, are clear in Table 16. Negro employment at best barely

22. *Business Week,* June 22, 1963, p. 44.
23. *Ibid.,* p. 46.

TABLE 17. *Aerospace Industry, Employment by Race, Sex, and Region*
23 Companies, 179 Establishments, 1964

Region	All Employees			Male			Female		
	Total	Negro	Percent Negro	Total	Negro	Percent Negro	Total	Negro	Percent Negro
Northeast	145,535	3,660	2.5	127,448	3,339	2.6	18,087	321	1.8
New England	77,373	1,648	2.1	66,912	1,533	2.3	10,461	115	1.1
Middle Atlantic	68,162	2,012	3.0	60,536	1,806	3.0	7,626	206	2.7
South	103,827	2,903	2.8	90,598	2,627	2.9	13,229	276	2.1
Southeast	57,764	2,068	3.6	50,521	1,846	3.7	7,243	222	3.1
Southwest	46,063	835	1.8	40,077	781	1.9	5,986	54	0.9
Midwest	93,414	3,862	4.1	82,596	3,604	4.4	10,818	258	2.4
West Coast	311,772	9,634	3.1	253,673	7,906	3.1	58,099	1,728	3.0
Southern California	216,474	8,108	3.7	173,011	6,650	3.8	43,463	1,458	3.4
Other West Coast	95,298	1,526	1.6	80,662	1,256	1.6	14,636	270	1.8
Total United States	654,548	20,059	3.1	554,315	17,476	3.2	100,233	2,583	2.6

Source: Data supplied to Plans for Progress.
Note: For geographic definitions, see Table 16.

held its own in this period despite special government and company efforts to open up new opportunities for minorities, and despite an overall increase of 100,000 in total aerospace employment from 1960 to 1963.

On a regional basis the 1963 data show Southern California, the Mid-Atlantic area (mostly New York and Philadelphia), and the Midwest continuing to have the highest percentage of Negro employment. The South continued to demonstrate a poor record in this regard.

In 1964, some improvement occurred in the Negro employment picture. The data in Table 17 include some plants which were not covered by the 1963 survey summarized in Table 16, but these differences do not account for the dramatic improvement in the Southeast and West Coast, which accounted for the bulk of the improvement. The most important action which contributed to the upturn in Negro employment was undoubtedly the heightened pressure to improve the Negro's position in industry. The major aircraft producers made notable progress in developing special programs to increase Negro employment. Aspects of these programs will be discussed in detail after the 1966 data are examined. The Southwest, still with a heavy backlog of layoffs, showed little progress in 1964.

The distribution of Negroes within broad occupational groups in 1964 is shown in Table 18. The usual concentration in the less skilled categories is again apparent. The relatively high proportion of craftsmen (skilled employees) does, however, indicate that upward movement in at least the factory was under way by this date.

THE GENERAL PICTURE AND "AFFIRMATIVE ACTION" SINCE 1966

Table 19 shows employment in the aerospace industry by occupational group, race, and sex for 21 companies and 127 establishments located in all regions of the country. The sample includes all major aerospace corporations and about 60 percent of the industry's labor force. It includes all major facilities covered by the data in Tables 16-18, omitting only some of the smaller plants reported therein.

The first significant fact revealed by the data in Table 19 is the continued expansion of Negro employment—almost 5 percent of total aerospace employees in 1966, and nearly twice the percentage revealed by the similar, but not completely comparable, data in Table

TABLE 18. *Aerospace Industry, Employment by Race, Sex, and Occupational Group, Total United States 23 Companies, 179 Establishments, 1964*

Occupational Group	All Employees			Male			Female		
	Total	Negro	Percent Negro	Total	Negro	Percent Negro	Total	Negro	Percent Negro
Officials and managers	60,541	172	0.3	59,895	169	0.3	646	3	0.5
Professionals	162,706	1,130	0.7	159,529	1,094	0.7	3,177	36	1.1
Technicians	56,363	929	1.6	51,658	876	1.7	4,705	53	1.1
Sales workers	887	1	0.1	852	1	0.1	35	—	—
Office and clerical	111,239	1,923	1.7	44,286	1,077	2.4	66,953	846	1.3
Craftsmen (Skilled)	132,402	3,826	2.9	128,571	3,674	2.9	3,831	152	4.0
Operatives (Semiskilled)	112,394	8,761	7.8	94,037	7,521	8.0	18,357	1,240	6.8
Laborers (Unskilled)	5,772	837	14.5	4,487	806	18.0	1,285	31	2.4
Service workers	12,244	2,480	20.3	11,000	2,258	20.5	1,244	222	17.8
Total	654,548	20,059	3.1	554,315	17,476	3.2	100,233	2,583	2.6

Source: Data supplied to Plans for Progress.

TABLE 19. *Aerospace Industry, Employment by Race, Sex, and Occupational Group, Total United States 21 Companies, 127 Establishments, 1966*

Occupational Group	All Employees			Male			Female		
	Total	Negro	Percent Negro	Total	Negro	Percent Negro	Total	Negro	Percent Negro
Officials and managers	71,328	292	0.4	70,638	289	0.4	690	3	0.4
Professionals	179,436	1,435	0.8	175,513	1,375	0.8	3,923	60	1.5
Technicians	63,999	1,209	1.9	57,284	1,128	2.0	6,715	81	1.2
Sales workers	720	2	0.3	673	2	0.3	47	—	—
Office and clerical	130,261	3,692	2.8	51,289	1,986	3.9	78,972	1,706	2.2
Craftsmen (Skilled)	164,991	7,595	4.6	158,623	7,050	4.4	6,368	545	8.6
Operatives (Semiskilled)	155,167	18,417	11.9	122,869	13,566	11.0	32,298	4,851	15.0
Laborers (Unskilled)	8,065	1,804	22.4	6,344	1,619	25.5	1,721	185	10.7
Service workers	14,055	3,124	22.2	12,015	2,792	23.2	2,040	332	16.3
Total	788,022	37,570	4.8	655,248	29,807	4.5	132,774	7,763	5.8

Source: Data in author's possession.

16. This is the highest percentage of Negroes found in any analysis of the industry's racial data heretofore. Moreover, it is likely that the percentage of Negroes in the industry has expanded since 1966. Continued expansion of aircraft production, and considerably less expansion in missile and space production, a tight labor market, and pressure by the government for "affirmative action" have all contributed to the expansion of Negro employment since 1964 and after 1966.

As already noted (see Figure 3, page 12), the great boom in commercial aviation and the needs of the armed services for helicopters, jet fighters, and bombers in Vietnam have all contributed to the expansion of the aircraft segment of the aerospace industry. The fact that aircraft production utilizes large numbers of semiskilled personnel whereas missile and space vehicle production requires a much higher complement of skilled workers and technical and professional personnel has been reiterated earlier. The production shift to aircraft and the tight labor market which has existed since 1965 have combined both to enhance Negro employment opportunities, and to give aerospace (as well as other) employers added incentive to find ways and means of utilizing Negroes and others whose training and background are below what was available in the looser labor markets of the late 1950's and early 1960's. Government and public policy to enhance employment opportunities for Negroes has thus been operating in what is fortuitously a favorable climate for success.

Affirmative action takes many forms. It involves such programs as recruiting in depressed areas like the Watts section of Los Angeles, developing special training programs for the disadvantaged, or simply giving preference in fact to Negroes. All the major Southern California aerospace firms, for example, set up special recruiting efforts in Watts after the 1965 riot there. Aerojet-General went further by establishing a tent-making subsidiary operated and manned by Negroes in the heart of Watts. Other companies financed training and motivational centers there. In addition, in late 1966, and early 1967, nearly 8,000 on-the-job trainees were enrolled in Southern California aerospace firms under the provisions of the federal Manpower Development and Training Act. Nearly all these trainees were classified as disadvantaged, and virtually all were Negroes or Mexicans.[24]

24. Letter to the author from Hugh C. Murphy, Administrator, Bureau of Apprenticeship and Training, U. S. Department of Labor, October 10, 1967.

In other areas, these special programs have also been pursued. United Aircraft's Pratt & Whitney division in Connecticut has made notable strides in rescuing dropouts and converting them through an elaborate training program into semiskilled or even skilled personnel. Pratt & Whitney has over 200 men and women in the training section of the personnel department, and had 7,000 persons in formal training in 1967 plus another 5,000 in a special short course.[25]

Boeing's Vertol division in Philadelphia has developed a careful, elaborate training program which has put many persons, including large numbers from the heavily Negro Chester, Pennsylvania, area into useful jobs, especially in its machine shop. McDonnell in St. Louis has among the highest proportion of Negroes in the industry in part because of its willingness to train those who might ordinarily be considered unemployable. Many other examples could be given of aerospace industry training and of special efforts to enroll Negroes in training courses.

Also in Philadelphia, General Electric's missile and space division has been a leading supporter of the Opportunities Industrialization Center, the much publicized self-help motivational and training institute, which has now been set up in over thirty other localities. Avco is building a plant in a Boston slum which will be operated and manned entirely by Negroes. General Dynamics, which is building the F-111 plane in Fort Worth, Texas, has established a satellite plant at San Antonio to train and to provide jobs for persons considered heretofore to be unemployable. Both the Avco facility which will employ 250 at full production, and that of General Dynamics which expects to have 200 jobs, are being established in collaboration with federal programs seeking to reduce hard-core, inner city unemployment.

All major aerospace companies are members of Plans for Progress, with Lockheed being the first company enrolled. Plans for Progress concerns are, in effect, committed to go beyond nondiscrimination, and to develop programs and activities designed to further the employment of Negroes and other minorities. This has involved such already noted programs as hiring and training hard-core unemployed, establishing work areas or plants in Negro slum areas, special recruit-

25. See Edward R. Cowles, "Rx for Shop Skills," United Aircraft, *Bee-Hive,* Vol. XXXXIII (January 1968), pp. 25-29, for the details of the Pratt & Whitney training program.

ment drives at Negro schools and colleges, and a host of other programs.

As the leading and largest government contractors, aerospace concerns are constantly being inspected by representatives of the various government procurement agencies, the Office of Federal Contract Compliance which now coordinates enforcement of the various Presidential Executive Orders relating to nondiscrimination by government contractors, the Equal Employment Opportunity Commission, and in many cases by state agencies as well. The obligations to take "affirmative action" are constantly before the aerospace companies, and they are usually the first to be "invited" to take part in new programs.

Pressure by the government has also resulted in companies literally giving preference to Negro applicants. Many leading aerospace concerns have told their employment interviewers that every effort should be made to hire Negroes who come even close to meeting minimum qualifications. Some have adopted an unwritten policy of outright preference: give the job to the Negro if he is available. One midwestern plant, where Negro employment was "disappointingly low" to the company's headquarters officials and to the government inspectors, hired 13.4 percent of its Negro applicants in the first seven months of 1967 as compared with 11.4 percent of its total applicants. Moreover, although total employment in this plant declined during this period, Negro employment increased even beyond the percentage increase resulting from the higher proportion of Negro recruits. This probably indicates some selection in layoffs to improve the percentage of Negroes on the payroll.

In one Southern California plant, which is located in a community where very few Negroes or Mexican-Americans dwell, the company moved to better its minority group employment (Mexican-Americans as well as Negroes) even though 10 percent of its 21,000 employees were from these groups. From November 1966 to August 1967, minority groups comprised 16.3 percent of all hires and were involved in 11.5 percent of all upgradings and promotions. Sixty percent of Negroes who applied were employed, but only 6 percent of the white persons who sought work were employed![26]

Numerous other examples could be cited of various types of

26. Data cited herein are from a variety of confidential sources, and have been carefully checked for accuracy.

"affirmative action." It is, for example, not uncommon for personnel executives to counsel with Negroes who have poor attendance or excessive tardiness records; or to approve several in-plant transfers for those who do not seem to be able to "get adjusted" to a supervisor; or otherwise to attempt to understand and to meet the problems of new Negro employees who seem unable to conform to the rules, regulations, or mores of the factory.

The executives of some companies have, of course, a greater commitment to equal employment opportunity than do those of others. For some it is a necessary order of business, to others, it is that plus a moral commitment. Within this framework, the author has not found any company of the twenty-one surveyed which was not making a real effort to expand Negro employment. Yet total Negro employment was less than 5 percent in 1966. This is approximately one-third of the proportion in the automobile industry and considerably less than that in many other industries. The reasons for this seeming paradox will be made clear after the ensuing discussion of occupational differences and intraplant movement of workers.

OFFICIALS AND MANAGERS

A feature of the present affirmative action campaign in the aerospace industry is the search for Negro managerial talent. The great bulk of the 292 Negroes listed as "officials and managers" in Table 19 are first-line supervisors. Aerospace companies have diligently searched their ranks for supervisory talent, and continue to do so. Some Negro supervisors preside over all Negro labor or janitorial gangs, but most are out on the line managing mixed crews. Despite their small number and percentage, there have been a sufficient number of breakthroughs so that Negroes deserving of promotion out of the ranks now obtain full and fair consideration, or occasionally even preference, for supervisory appointments.

Few Negroes now have middle or top management jobs in the aerospace industry—or in industry generally. Traditionally Negroes with talent, education, and motivation have not sought careers in business. The doors have been much more open in certain professions, particularly teaching, and to a lesser degree, medicine and the law. Now the barriers are lowered. The potential Negro executive is today assiduously pursued by business recruiters, and the aerospace companies are in the forefront of the pursuers. But the availability is very small. The prestigious business schools, conscious of their need to attract and to interest Negroes in graduate business study, have developed several programs to do so, but the success is limited. The number of Negroes trained, or training for, executive positions continues to remain very small. It will be many years before the Negro manager is a common occurrence in aerospace or in any other major industry. Few today are found above middle management; this author knows of none in the top ranks of the aerospace industry. Several are in the personnel function; some in the engineering middle management. The fact that the Negro middle manager is becoming more common, if still relatively rare, presages a continued upward movement, qualitatively and quantitatively, albeit slowly.

PROFESSIONALS, TECHNICIANS, AND SALES WORKERS

The professional group is the largest occupational category in the industry. Aerospace companies have scoured the country looking for professional and technical employees. Unfortunately, Negroes seeking professional education and attainment have only recently been welcomed into engineering work, and consequently few Negroes even today seek engineering degrees. Moreover, the engineering taught at many of the traditionally Negro colleges is often substandard in general, but particularly inferior for the aerospace industry whose professionals are so often asked to develop products never heretofore made.

Nevertheless, most aerospace companies have their Negro engineer success stories (usually shown in pictures in the annual report!). Aerospace may well have as large, if not the largest, supply of Negro engineers of any industry, as it has of white engineers. Many companies in the industry have been recruiting Negro engineers for a long period, some as far back as World War II. A number do indeed have Negroes who are key members of their professional group. A Negro engineer who is available today can count on attractive job offers, both in terms of money and of the character of the work, from almost every major aerospace concern that learns of his availability. The unfortunate effect, of course, of years of discrimination is that so few Negroes can qualify as engineers.

Technicians are somewhat similarly situated in so far as Negro employment is concerned. Their technical training is the result either of school work somewhat below the engineering level, or they have advanced by experience and/or special training up from the ranks of shop craftsmen. In either case, they have backgrounds of work or training from which few Negroes were once admitted and for which few Negroes are now trained. Nevertheless, real progress has been made in this area. There are quite a few first-rate Negro technicians in aerospace plants, some of whom came up through the ranks over the years. But here again, future prospects are good only if the Negro population can become convinced of the potential which technical education promises. The jobs are there, but the obstacles to achieve the jobs remain formidable, as our discussion of the craftsmen situation, below, will again emphasize.

As has already been noted, few employees in the aerospace industry are classified as sales personnel, and those few are usually private plane salesmen or other specialty marketing personnel. A major distributor of one of the largest private plane manufacturing companies is a Negro. His salesmen and sales agencies are largely white and he is reputed to be very successful. Selling to the government, or to the major airlines, is a job calling for the designation of an executive, manager, or professional in so far as the aerospace industry is concerned. Whatever the designation, few Negroes are so employed. This is the practice throughout American industry, a practice that must change with the times. It will be instructive indeed, as the aerospace industry moves with the times, as it must, and utilizes Negroes in sales, marketing, sales engineering, and customer contact work, to observe how such changes are accepted by the industry's prime contractor, the government.

OFFICE AND CLERICAL

Despite some major progress, Negroes comprised only 2.8 percent of the clerical employees for 1966 in the Table 19 data. This reflects, among other aspects, the late start at which Negroes were accepted as office workers in the industry. The office and clerical group is the fourth largest in the industry, comprising 16.5 percent of the total work force. It not only offers a multitude of jobs, but includes many such as purchasing clerks, bookkeepers, personnel assistants, etc., from which promotion into lower-management ranks is customary.

In recent years, aerospace companies have made strenuous efforts to expand their Negro clerical work forces. They have sponsored special training programs, visited and recruited at predominantly

Negro high schools, and taken graduates of special training groups, such as those sponsored by community human relations commissions, Urban Leagues, or the Opportunities Industrialization Centers. Two prime reasons for their inability to expand their Negro clerical percentage are lack of training and background and the locational factor.

Just as the segregated schools of the South and those in the inner city core are relatively deficient in their mathematics training, so they are in English grammar, punctuation, and spelling. The girl who graduates from such an institution and is told that she is a typist receives a rude shock when she is tested in an industrial setting. Her speed is likely to be substandard, but practice can overcome that. What is more serious is that she is likely to be a poor speller, have little idea of proper punctuation, and have had inferior training in how to set up a memorandum or business letter.

Aerospace industry officials—and most others—would often prefer to train high school graduates initially, rather than have to retrain them. The girl who thinks that she has learned stenography often resents being retaught and feels discriminated against because she is unaware how lacking in skills she actually is. As one personnel officer told the author: "When we suggest that we are willing to train a girl at our expense, she is sometimes outraged and files a case of discrimination with the state or the federal Equal Opportunity Commission. Inevitably, the record of her typing and English test exonerates us. But in the meantime, we have spent hours proving that we did not discriminate, lost a potential employee whom we need, and hurt our image with the friends and neighbors of the girl."[27]

The locational problem is a serious one which will be discussed in greater detail below. Suffice it here to point out that most aerospace facilities are located on the outskirts of cities and cannot be reached except by private car. Even, however, where public transportation exists, the travel problem remains a significant factor in reducing Negro participation in the industry and especially, the participation of Negro women. Studies of the author in other industries have confirmed the fact that, even where men are willing to travel long distances to work, women seeking work in an office are not.[28] Neighborhoods in which Negroes are concentrated are usually

27. Interview, Los Angeles, January 1967.
28. See, for example, Herbert R. Northrup, *The Negro in the Automobile Industry* (Philadelphia: University of Pennsylvania, Industrial Research Unit, 1968). Racial Policies in American Industry, Report No. 1, pp. 45-46.

long distances from aerospace facilities. As a result, qualified Negro women tend to gravitate toward office and clerical work in the nearby center cities. Until Negroes can or do find housing in the outer city and suburbs, the aerospace industry's search for more Negro office and clerical employees will have only limited success.

THE CRAFTSMEN PROBLEM

Craftsmen is a broad designation in the aerospace industry. It includes maintenance and machine setup men, tool and die workers, machinists, electricians, millwrights, and others typically found in this category. It also includes some persons engaged in what is essentially assembly work. And it includes mechanics with great capability and versatility in electro-mechanical, hydraulics, pneumatics, or combinations of all three, as well as many other highly or even uniquely skilled workers.

During the past two decades, there has been a tremendous upgrading of skills in the industry. According to the Vice-President of Industrial Relations of Lockheed, "an amazing upward . . . shift in job skills occurred. . . . In 1944, what might be called the 'normal labor market' could fill more than 80 percent of the workforce needs (operatives and low-skilled). Today less than half these jobs can be filled from that market. Even more critical is the sharp cutback of low-skilled jobs—those that might normally be filled by 'almost anyone.' A generation ago more than half the jobs were in this category. Today less than one-quarter are, and the number of workers at the craft level has about tripled."[29]

If this change in skill composition is critical for labor and management, it is even more so for Negro labor. Obtaining skilled blue collar work has always been difficult for Negroes in all industry. The craft unions in the building and metal trades have been historically, continually, and almost universally antagonistic to acceptance of Negroes as apprentices in areas of work under their control.[30] Small businessmen in these trades are frequently former craftsmen who share the racial outlook of their onetime colleagues, but who, in any case, are in no position to oppose the unions on such questions or often, even to train many apprentices.

29. J. D. Hodgson, "The No-Longer-So-Blue-Collar Worker," address at the IRC Management Course, Williamsburg, Va., November 8, 1967, p. 3.
30. For background on this problem, see Northrup, *Organized Labor and the Negro*, Chapter 2.

Negroes desirous of seeking employment leading to skilled blue collar work also cannot as easily short-circuit formal training as can many white workers. The latter often have the opportunity to work as aids or helpers to friends, neighbors, or relatives who work at a trade. Except in the southern trowel trades (bricklaying, plastering, or cement finishing), where a tradition of Negro participation has existed since slavery days, the Negro aspiring to skilled work finds few members of his race already in the trade and therefore able to aid him, and few whites willing to do so.

As a result, Negroes aiming at craftsmen's work find their best opportunities with those large employers, who have the need and financial resources to train and to upgrade their work force and who are expected as a social obligation, and now as a matter of law or public policy, to make certain that Negroes participate in that training and upgrading. Of course, the aerospace industry fits this description as well as, if not better than, most others. Moreover, the aerospace industry has probably done as good a job, if not a better one, than most industries in recruiting, training, and upgrading Negroes to the craftsmen level. The percentage of Negro craftsmen shown in Table 19 is approximately equal to the percentage of Negroes in the industry—4.6 percent craftsmen, 4.8 percent total Negro. The author knows of no other major industry where Negro representation at the skilled level equals total representation.

Of course one may look at these data in an adverse way—that the overall recruitment level of Negroes is poor. The thrust of this analysis, however, is that the relatively low participation of Negroes in the aerospace industry is, above all, a function of the skill requirements of the industry. The rate of Negro participation in the industry is substantially reduced by the low percentage of Negroes in the salaried areas. In this aerospace is not unique, but rather typical of American industry. Since, however, professionals are the largest occupational category in the industry, comprising 22.8 percent of the total industry labor force, and since white collar and salaried employees make up 56.6 percent of the industry labor force, total Negro participation in the industry is affected in a major way by the lack of Negro representation in these occupational groups. Under the circumstances, Negro participation in the craftsmen group is relatively high, although certainly less than one-half the Negro population ratio in the country.

Among the other factors which keep Negro participation in aerospace craftsmen work from rising at a more rapid rate is of course educational deficiencies among Negro youth. Segregated southern schools and those in the inner city slums of northern cities provide inferior educational backgrounds particularly in communication skills and mathematics than do the white southern, or outer city or suburban schools which few Negroes attend. The large school drop-out rates of Negroes accelerate this problem. The lack of Negro family industrial background in industry and skilled craft work, the demoralized Negro family structure with its missing father, and until recently, the predominant feeling that aspiration to skilled industrial work was not a practical hope, have all reduced the availability of Negroes for skilled work.

To offset these problems, the aerospace companies have made special efforts to recruit Negro apprenticeship candidates. The results have not been encouraging. Close contacts with high schools have uncovered far too few Negroes with the interest and mathematics background or capability. Those on the margin of mathematics competence have been offered special courses or tutoring by several companies, with very limited success in either enrollment or course completion. The Negro who qualifies in mathematics is now firmly college-oriented and is likely also to be uninterested in an apprentice course.

As a result of the historical problems of discrimination, the Negro aerospace craftsman, like his professional counterpart, is disproportionately found in the lower echelons of his group. Proportionately many fewer Negroes are tool and die workers, top-rated machinists, electromechanical, hydraulic, or pneumatic mechanics than are whites. Negro craftsmen are more heavily concentrated in less sophisticated sheet metal, pipe, millwright, or bench mechanic operations. Many of the latter have worked up from semiskilled operatives.

Such upgrading is the prime source of Negro craftsmen today. Many have come into the industry as unskilled employees and now are craftsmen with high-rated jobs. The aerospace industry is probably the most training conscious industry in America. Given the fantastically changing technology which underlies its products, it can do little without continous training. Most companies post training notices throughout plants and personnel departments constantly urging employees to take training courses, and thereby helping companies solve the skill shortages. In recent years, special efforts have been made to encourage Negroes to take advantage of training pro-

TABLE 20. *Three Case Histories of Training and Results, Aerospace Industry*

1 *John R - - - -*	2 *Porter P - - - -*	3 *Robert H - - - -*
John R is a Negro. He applied in 1960 and at the time was 28 years old, married and had been working as a garage mechanic "on commission." He was a high school graduate (South Carolina) and had been a mechanic in military service.	Porter P is a Negro. He applied in 1955. At the time he was 22 years old, married and had been working locally as a farm laborer. He had attended high school for two years in Alabama.	Robert H is a Negro. He was 28 and single in 1961 when he applied. He was a high school graduate (Norwich, Conn.). He had resigned as a "pilot and mechanic" from a Groton, Connecticut flight organization.
He was hired as a 3-week machine operator trainee at $2.00 per hour.	He was employed as a parts washer in October 1955. This job was the division's second lowest labor grade —yet it paid 27c per hour more than he had been earning.	He was hired in 1961 as an Engine Assembly Inspector "B" at $2.37 per hour.
		He was promoted that same year and his rate increased to $2.44 per hour.
Three years later, in 1963, he was accepted into the 26-week Production Machining course. Upon graduation in January of 1964, he was paid $2.57 per hour.	In 1959 he was enrolled in the 26-week Production Machining course and graduated in May of 1960 at $2.29 per hour.	In 1962 he was selected to attend the Jet Engine Familiarization course—a less than 8 hour course. Later in 1962 he was again promoted and his rate had risen to $2.93 per hour.
He received promotions in 1964 and 1965. The 1965 promotion was to Leadman and his rate of pay had risen to $2.84 per hour.	In 1961 he received a two grade promotion with a rate of $2.42 per hour.	In 1964 he was demoted one grade as a consequence of a work force reduction— but regained the lost grade by the end of the year.
Currently he is paid $3.33 per hour.	In 1966 he received a two grade promotion and his hourly rate was $3.10.	

	2 *Porter P - - - -*	3 *Robert H - - - -*
	In July of this year he was again promoted two labor grades to the second highest labor grade for non-supervisory employees. His rate is $3.52 per hour.	In 1965 he attended the following Training School courses: Magnaflux Inspection 30 hours X-Ray Inspection 30 hours Quality Assurance Changes 20 hours Basic Layout Inspection 400 hours In 1966 he was promoted one grade and his base rate reached $3.43 per hour. In 1966 he also attended the following Training School courses: Alloy Type Testing 14 hours Visual Inspection 12 hours Foreman Candidate Training 120 hours In 1966 he was promoted to Foreman. His salary was the equivalent of $3.83 per hour. This year, 1967, as a foreman he has attended the following Training School courses: Statistical Quality Control for Supervisors 20 hours Fluorescent Penetrant Inspection 16 hours His current salary is the equivalent of $4.43 per hour.

Source: Company files.

grams. What can happen when they do is set forth in three case histories in Table 20.

Unfortunately, Negro participation in training is almost universally below the proportion of Negroes in a plant. Motivational factors appear very important. Willingness to contribute one's time to train for a better future depends on background, expectations, and genuine belief in opportunity. That all three are lacking to some degree in the Negro community is not difficult to understand. There is also undoubtedly some reluctance on the part of Negroes in plants to do anything which would transfer them from a job situation which appears acceptable to white fellow workers to one which may not be. Some Negroes (and of course whites, too) are making more money than they ever expected. They see no need to spend time learning new skills, especially in a volatile industry where the end of a contract, or of hostilities in Vietnam, could bring a layoff. Yet until training opportunities are fully grasped, Negro upgrading will not achieve its great potential in the aerospace industry.

OPERATIVES

The operative jobs vary widely from some rather close tolerance assembly work to essentially entry jobs. The operative group was traditionally the largest occupational category in the aircraft and parts industry, and still is in the manufacture of engines and aircraft. In the overall aerospace industry, however, the number of craftsmen now exceeds the number of operatives. In missile and space work, the number of craftsmen greatly exceeds that of operatives.

Negroes hold about the same proportion of operatives jobs in the aerospace industry as their proportion to the general population. Their operative representation is also more than twice that of their representation in the industry as a whole. Again, within the operative group, there is a tendency for Negroes to be disproportionately concentrated in the lower-rated sectors.

The aerospace companies which have both missile and space and aircraft work have a much higher percentage of Negroes in the latter. Aircraft engine factories also usually feature a higher proportion of Negroes than do missile and space facilities operating in the same area or region. The reasons, of course, are the character of work and the training and educational backgrounds of Negro applicants.

Assembly line work exists in aircraft factories, but it is far different than automobile assembly line operations. An aircraft company that produces one plane per day for a year or two is operating volume production by the standards of its industry. Automobile assembly plants are geared to produce up to sixty vehicles per hour. The aircraft jobs are not nearly as broken down as are those in the automobile industry. The latter industry can take unskilled persons off the street, and with little or no training start them on the assembly line.[31] This cannot be done in aerospace. The assembly line work is much more complicated, and the cost of mistakes is too great to risk inadequate training. Before new applicants are put onto the line, they must have careful training, varying from a few weeks to several months. Life is involved, and the quality of workmanship cannot be compromised.

All major companies which have lower-rated semiskilled work have elaborate introductory or vestibule training programs. Some now even teach shop mores and manners—how to dress, use sanitary facilities, and live under shop regimentation—as well as the basic fundamentals of workmanship before taking up the rudimentary components of work to be done. From such programs, there is usually a high initial drop-out rate, but those that remain often become useful workers, and many advance up the occupational ladder.

The future of Negroes in the aerospace operative category is largely tied to the expansion of aircraft production. A combination of tremendous commercial expansion and the needs of the Vietnam war for combat aircraft and helicopters has created a tight labor market. Companies now have to train workers for entry jobs in most areas in order to obtain any labor, and Negroes have profited immensely from this situation. Layoffs would hit them hard as their seniority is less as a group than whites. Until, however, aircraft production slows down, one may expect continued expansion of Negro representation among aerospace industry operatives.

LABORERS AND SERVICE WORKERS

Not many employees in aerospace are found in the "laborer" category—about 1 percent of the total labor force. They are low-rated employees who do odd jobs around the plants and offices, but do not work in production. Negroes make up a far disproportionate

31. For details, see the work cited in note 28, *supra*.

share of this small group in aerospace as they do in all industry. For the Negro (or white) with little education, ability, or indeed prospects, these jobs offer a livelihood. Their insignificant number in aerospace, however, attests both to the nature of work in the industry, and the declining opportunity for those with little skills or potential. The unskilled person with reasonable potential and motivation today in aerospace need not even start as a laborer, but in most cases, can move directly into training for work in the operative category.

Service workers entail a wider occupational grouping and make up about 2 percent of the labor force in the industry, with Negroes again highly disproportionately represented. They include porters, messengers, cafeteria workers, and if not classified as laborers, groundskeepers and janitors—all jobs traditionally open to Negroes, and usually dead-end jobs. Also included in this grouping are plant guards, a larger group in aerospace than in most industries because of classified work and security problems. In many areas, Negroes were denied the opportunity to work as plant guards until very recently. The rationale seems to have been that Negro guards would have difficulty handling problems affecting white personnel. This reasoning was maintained long after Negro police officers and officers in the armed services lost their novelty. There is still underrepresentation of Negroes among plant guards, but no longer are they denied opportunities in this classification as a matter of course.

NEGRO WOMEN IN AEROSPACE

The aerospace industry became a large employer of Negro women during World War II, and the tradition has continued, especially in Southern California. Substantial gains have been made in the utilization of Negro women in the shop in recent years. They comprise in the Table 19 sample 8.6 percent of the 6,368 women classified as craftsmen and 15 percent of the 32,298 female operatives.

One reason for the increased use of women, and therefore also of Negro women, is the large amount of electrical and electronic assembly work in modern aerospace technology. Thousands of wires and circuits wend their way through the structures of aircraft, missiles, and space vehicles. Women are especially adept at such small assembly work and are extensively used for it. As the labor market tightened and civil rights pressures increased, Negro women increased their share of such work.

Recent years have also seen an increased utilization of Negro women in sheet metal assembly in aircraft plants and as grinders, welders, and small machine tool operators in engine plants. Several companies have had better experience with Negro women than Negro men in these jobs, particularly women with families. The tradition of female family support seems to generate a strong determination to take advantage of opportunities in the Negro women employed by these aerospace firms. In one such case, a plant manager bitterly opposed using Negro women until forced to do so by the company president. Later he was so pleased with the results that he had to be stopped from issuing an order requesting preference for Negro women.

There is still some reluctance to use Negro women in the shop—indeed a few plants have no women—but if the labor market continues to be tight, this will probably change. Perhaps since shop work is not available in the inner city, as is office work, Negro women who work in blue collar jobs are apparently more willing to travel than are female office workers. It is nevertheless quite likely that the distance of most aerospace plants from Negro communities tends to reduce considerably the availability of Negro women for the industry's plant labor force.

INTRAPLANT MOVEMENT AND SENIORITY

The seniority systems in aerospace are quite varied, but in general do not seem to restrict Negro intraplant movement. There are some dead-end jobs. In a few companies, not necessarily in the South, laborers and janitors are outside any normal progression. Employees with any considered potential are hired in as operatives, usually in the light electronic or sheet metal assembly. Because job bidding is so prevalent, however, a laborer with qualification or potential can move out of his classification.

Most seniority districts tend to be broad with families of jobs clustered in one district. There are occasional plant-wide applications, and in some situations, transfers among plants of one company are part of the collective agreement. In a few cases, seniority lines are long and narrow, making it difficult to break into a job category, but these are not as common as the job cluster type in which a large group of job families provide the potential for movement on a broad front without transferring out of a seniority district, and therefore suffering loss of existing job seniority in order to obtain a better job.

It should be emphasized that in the aerospace industry, the dynamic technology makes seniority far more important in layoffs than in promotions. Qualification is so important that training and ability are far more significant than length of service. The failure of Negroes to take full advantage of training opportunities hurts their progress. In an industry in which qualification cannot be shaded, and one in which the opportunities for training are almost endless, these opportunities must be grasped if equal opportunity is to be assured.

In general, the wider the seniority district, the greater the opportunity for Negroes for upgrading and advancement. As the most recently hired and the group which has the fewest skills, Negroes profit substantially from broad opportunities for movement. But, of course, a wide seniority progression system has its corollary disadvantages, too. When employment turns downward, it provides the broadest opportunities for bumping. With Negroes both relatively new and still overly concentrated in the semiskilled and relatively unskilled jobs, they are then especially vulnerable.

Job bidding is widely used in the industry to fill higher jobs. Company officials have repeatedly complained to the author that Negroes appear more reluctant to bid on jobs than do whites, and that Negroes often require great encouragement if they are to bid. The situation is similar to the already noted disproportionate reluctance of Negroes to take advantage of training opportunities. Again the reasons appear to be lack of experience in industrial practices, fear of moving from a job situation which is acceptable to white fellow workers to one which is not, or lack of motivation.

Attempts to promote Negroes to supervisory ranks also sometimes run into unexpected opposition. Refusal to accept such promotion is, of course, not unique in industrial experience. Many white workers prefer the more placid existence of an hourly employee to the responsibilities, frustrations, and pressures of the supervisor. Companies have, however, reported to the author in a number of cases that promotion was declined because it carried an "Uncle Tom" connotation, or because it meant a break with "Black Power" psychology. Apparently, in such instances a supervisory job was considered by the man's peers to be synonymous with going over to the white enemy. In one case, it was all quite puzzling to the employer who had been charged previously with discrimination for not elevating a Negro to supervisor.

In general, intraplant movement is affected by the same factors which affect Negro job opportunities generally. Basic, of course, is an expanding economy. Unless jobs are available, upward movement is difficult, and jobs held by Negroes can be lost. The supply side of Negro labor is, however, deeply disadvantaged by inferior education, training, and experience. The aerospace industry must require skill and educational attainments that disproportionately few Negroes possess, and there cannot be legitimate compromise with these requirements. Acquiring skills and education is a time-consuming process. Upward job movement of Negroes in this industry is, therefore, likely to continue to lag as long as the Negro educational and skill gap endures, even though the industry may offset the lag somewhat by its massive training program.

Negro job movement up the occupational ladder is also adversely affected by the locational factors, discussed in the next section, and directly affected by government policies which are examined in the last sector of this chapter. Union policies, as we shall point out, are relatively passive.

Discrimination and motivation go hand in hand. Because of the former, the latter is often lacking. Opportunities for promotion, for training, or for improvement are not grasped. The promotion process is thus slowed and discrimination often charged. Inexperience in industry, lack of help in setting goals, and the difficulty of breaking with the past all combine to resist upward job movement.

LOCATIONAL FACTORS

Although the aerospace industry is located in all regions of the country and near virtually every major center of Negro population, the nature of the industry requires plant site locations that are unfavorable to Negro employment. This is the result of a combination of circumstances: aerospace products are likely to need ample space for testing, which is not available within cities; but Negroes are more and more concentrated in center city inner cores and have difficulty finding housing in suburbs or towns near aircraft plants; and public transportation is not usually adequate to offset these factors.

Consider, for example, the situation in St. Louis. Since 1950, a quarter of a million whites have moved out of the city proper and an even greater number of Negroes have taken their place, so that now almost 40 percent of the city's population is Negro. The Negroes are concentrated on the so-called North Side. As in most cities, manufacturing employment has declined, many industries having moved to the predominantly white, fast growing suburbs.[32] A recent article in *Fortune* commented:

> The decline of industry in the city has been a bitter development for the North Side, where a survey found unemployment running above 12 percent late in 1966. Expanding employment in the county has provided relatively few jobs for city dwellers. At its huge plant seventeen miles from the North Side, McDonnell Douglas, by far the biggest employer in the metropolitan area, has actively recruited and trained St. Louis Negroes. But though McDonnell's work force has swelled from 22,000 to 42,000 since 1960, the company still employs fewer than 5,000 St. Louisans. The proportion of city residents on the payroll has actually slumped since 1960, from 17 to 12 percent.
>
> One employment obstacle for North Side people is the lack of direct public transportation to where the suburban jobs are. It takes as much as two hours, and three buses, to get from the North Side to the McDonnell plant. Later this year, with the help of a federal grant, the city will be starting a direct bus service, probably from the North Side to the McDonnell area. But the number of industrial jobs out there for unskilled and semiskilled city people is much smaller than the number of unemployed North Siders. Scattered around in the suburbs are quite a few service jobs that North Siders could fill, but the wages are generally not high enough to make up for the long trip.[33]

The situation described here is typical of the locational problem of the industry. In Southern California, for example, where the greatest concentration of aerospace work is found, there are many towns in which Negroes are unable to obtain housing. Transportation is almost impossible from the heavily populated Negro areas of Los Angeles to some of the major aerospace facilities located in these towns or in the counties outside of Los Angeles. The plants located either close to the areas in Los Angeles, such as Watts, where Negroes are concentrated, or on the few direct public transportation routes from these areas, generally have two or three times the proportion of Negroes that those plants have which are located in the outer county areas, even though the same companies and the same

32. "The St. Louis Economic Blues," *Fortune,* Vol. LXXVII (January 1968), pp. 210-211.
33. *Ibid.,* p. 210.

policies are involved. Despite intensive recruiting of Negroes, attempts to aid in the establishment of car pools, and even subsidizing of public transport, the outlying plants find that turnover of Negroes who have long distances to commute is very high.

The public transportation situation is unlikely to improve. Buses serving slum areas have become so much a target for violence that it is difficult both to obtain bus drivers and to provide a service. Employees of the company serving the Watts area of Los Angeles threatened to strike until they received more police protection, and union officials throughout the county have been concerned about the problem.[34]

Self-help Negro groups have tried operating buses in both Los Angeles and New York to carry people to work.[35] It is too early to assess the results of their work, but it is unlikely that these efforts can succeed without subsidy. Companies are often willing to provide that subsidy, and have in many cities. Usually, however, the buses do not attract many riders. Those who remain at work obtain automobiles; others drop out because of a long commuting distance or for other reasons; only a few both stay at work and ride the bus.

As was noted early, long commutes are an almost insuperable barrier for female office workers. It is very difficult for aerospace plants to attract Negro office workers, and will remain so until the American housing pattern is changed, and suburban living is more accessible to Negroes.

Even if open housing legislation materially reduces discrimination against Negroes seeking housing, Negro movement to the suburbs and therefore closer to aerospace plants is not likely to be rapid. Suburban housing frequently requires an income that Negroes are much less able than whites to possess. Given the facts of education and background, the Negro income gap will not easily or quickly be closed. Moreover, most Negroes are, like all groups in society, likely to desire to migrate to, and to reside near, their own kind rather than to risk social rebuffs or isolation in locations where few of their race reside.

Interestingly enough, in the Southern California area particularly, many of the outlying plants which have much fewer Negroes than those closer to areas of Los Angeles where Negroes are concentrated,

---

34. See, e.g., the Victor Riesel syndicated column of December 18, 1967; and *New York Times,* November 26, 28, and 29, 1967.
35. *New York Times,* November 26, 1967, and January 3-4, 1968.

also have a much less skewed in-plant distribution of Negroes. These outlying plants are, with some significant exceptions like the Lockheed major facilities at Burbank, either new or newly integrated. In such plants, the practice of confining Negroes to low-skilled jobs never existed, and was easier to avoid than it was to overcome where it had become institutionalized. In addition, Negroes who do find a home in the suburbs or outer county areas, or who are willing to commute long distances, are usually both well qualified for their jobs and highly motivated. They are, therefore, capable both of finding work and of gaining promotion and upgrading opportunities.

Nevertheless, despite some exceptions, the farther from center city is the aerospace plant, the fewer Negroes are found on its employment rolls. Workers who have had little experience, motivation, or assistance do not know enough to look for work at a great distance. The expense of long commutes cuts deep into the income from low-skilled and entry jobs, and the frustrations of getting to work that is far from home easily discourage the inexperienced or uninitiated commuter. Moreover, superior workers can often find work closer to home. Consequently, both employment and upward job movement in the industry are restricted by the necessities of plant location, and its typical distance from the central city where Negroes are more and more concentrated.

REGIONAL DIFFERENCES — GENERAL

Tables 21-26 show Negro employment in the aerospace industry by occupational groups for all major regions of the country in 1966 except for the South, which is discussed in the following section. These tables utilize the same data which are summarized in Table 19, but divide them on a regional basis by establishment. Many companies are thus represented by plants in several regions.

Turning first to the Northeast (Table 21), we find Negro employment ratios and in-plant distributions fairly close to national averages throughout the entire occupational hierarchy. In this region, Negro females have a higher ratio of jobs than the industry's national average, and Negroes are somewhat less concentrated in the bottom two categories. They are, however, also less well represented in the craftsmen category, but hold almost an identical share of the salaried positions as they do nationally.

The Northeast region is divided into two areas, New England

TABLE 21. *Aerospace Industry, Employment by Race, Sex, and Occupational Group, Northeast Region, 1966*

	All Employees			Male			Female		
Occupational Group	Total	Negro	Percent Negro	Total	Negro	Percent Negro	Total	Negro	Percent Negro
Officials and managers	13,740	50	0.4	13,605	49	0.4	135	1	0.7
Professionals	34,604	247	0.7	34,027	242	0.7	577	5	0.9
Technicians	13,287	255	1.9	12,121	234	1.9	1,166	21	1.8
Sales workers	174	—	—	172	—	—	2	—	—
Office and clerical	21,575	571	2.6	8,193	245	3.0	13,382	326	2.4
Craftsmen (Skilled)	35,073	1,165	3.3	34,592	1,079	3.1	481	86	17.9
Operatives (Semiskilled)	42,188	4,554	10.8	35,626	3,312	9.3	6,562	1,242	18.9
Laborers (Unskilled)	3,988	563	14.1	2,958	474	16.0	1,030	89	8.6
Service workers	4,174	791	19.0	3,656	727	19.9	518	64	12.4
Total	168,803	8,196	4.9	144,950	6,362	4.4	23,853	1,834	7.7

Source: Data in author's possession.

Note: For geographic definitions, see Table 16, p. 32.

TABLE 22. *Aerospace Industry, Employment by Race, Sex, and Occupational Group, New England Region, 1966*

Occupational Group	All Employees			Male			Female		
	Total	Negro	Percent Negro	Total	Negro	Percent Negro	Total	Negro	Percent Negro
Officials and managers	8,121	29	0.4	8,052	29	0.4	69	—	—
Professionals	17,689	54	0.3	17,420	53	0.3	269	1	0.4
Technicians	6,098	53	0.9	5,259	40	0.8	839	13	1.5
Sales workers	170	—	—	168	—	—	2	—	—
Office and clerical	11,177	192	1.7	3,491	65	1.9	7,686	127	1.7
Craftsmen (Skilled)	18,366	357	1.9	18,301	341	1.9	65	16	24.6
Operatives (Semiskilled)	34,681	3,946	11.4	28,622	2,761	9.6	6,059	1,185	19.6
Laborers (Unskilled)	3,329	382	11.5	2,422	310	12.8	907	72	7.9
Service workers	2,001	198	9.9	1,689	159	9.4	312	39	12.5
Total	101,632	5,211	5.1	85,424	3,758	4.4	16,208	1,453	9.0

Source: Data in author's possession.

Note: For geographic definitions, see Table 16, p. 32.

TABLE 23. *Aerospace Industry, Employment by Race, Sex, and Occupational Group, Middle Atlantic Region, 1966*

	All Employees			Male			Female		
Occupational Group	Total	Negro	Percent Negro	Total	Negro	Percent Negro	Total	Negro	Percent Negro
Officials and managers	5,619	21	0.4	5,553	20	0.4	66	1	1.5
Professionals	16,915	193	1.1	16,607	189	1.1	308	4	1.3
Technicians	7,189	202	2.8	6,862	194	2.8	327	8	2.4
Sales workers	4	—	—	4	—	—	—	—	—
Office and clerical	10,398	379	3.6	4,702	180	3.8	5,696	199	3.5
Craftsmen (Skilled)	16,707	808	4.8	16,291	738	4.5	416	70	16.8
Operatives (Semiskilled)	7,507	608	8.1	7,004	551	7.9	503	57	11.3
Laborers (Unskilled)	659	181	27.5	536	164	30.6	123	17	13.8
Service workers	2,173	593	27.3	1,967	568	28.9	206	25	12.1
Total	67,171	2,985	4.4	59,526	2,604	4.4	7,645	381	5.0

Source: Data in author's possession.

Note: For geographic definitions, see Table 16, p. 32.

(Table 22) and Middle Atlantic (Table 23). The high proportion of operatives in New England is attributable to the location there of major engine plants of United Aircraft, Avco, and General Electric, which utilize a much higher proportion of such labor than do many other aerospace plants. The Negro representation here is very similar to the national average, but the high proportion of operatives offsets the lag of Negroes in the craftsmen classification and raises the overall Negro percentage to slightly above 5 percent. Negro women make up an even larger percentage of female employment in New England than they do in the total Northeast area. A heavy migration of Negroes from both the South and from New York City particularly to cities in Connecticut has been a strong factor in the increased representation of Negroes in New England aerospace plants. In addition, United Aircraft, the region's major aerospace employer, has long had a deserved reputation for practicing equal employment, a factor which, with opportunities of good jobs at high wages, has attracted many Negroes to jobs in the area.

The Middle Atlantic data (Table 23) again hold close to the national average in all categories. Female employment of Negroes is considerably less than in New England, but the type of work which predominates does not offer the same opportunities. In the Middle Atlantic Region, craftsmen outnumber operatives, two to one; in New England, the ratios are almost reversed. Large missile and space operations and considerable job and machine work are found in this area. The once great aircraft production facilities of Martin-Marietta near Baltimore have been greatly reduced, and with them, have gone numerous semiskilled jobs of which Negroes once held a good share. Boeing's Vertol Division near Philadelphia employs a large number of both craftsmen and operatives, and has done a very capable job of training and upgrading Negroes in the machining skills. The higher than average craftsmen representation of Negroes in this area testifies to the results of such programs.

The Midwest (Table 24) has the highest percentage of Negroes of any area—6.8 as compared with 4.8 nationwide. Since the data also include the few installations in the Rocky Mountain and Northern Plains areas, where few Negroes live, the data in Table 24, if anything, understate Negro representation in the traditional Midwest area.

The three great aerospace employment locations in the Midwest are Evendale, near Cincinnati, Ohio, where General Electric has its

TABLE 24. *Aerospace Industry, Employment by Race, Sex, and Occupational Group, Midwest Region, 1966*

Occupational Group	All Employees			Male			Female		
	Total	Negro	Percent Negro	Total	Negro	Percent Negro	Total	Negro	Percent Negro
Officials and managers	11,231	73	0.6	11,148	73	0.7	83	—	—
Professionals	18,318	146	0.8	17,941	140	0.8	377	6	1.6
Technicians	8,160	129	1.6	7,528	123	1.6	632	6	0.9
Sales workers	120	2	1.7	117	2	1.7	3	—	—
Office and clerical	18,723	639	3.4	9,690	464	4.8	9,033	175	1.9
Craftsmen (Skilled)	32,697	2,043	6.2	31,454	1,929	6.1	1,243	114	9.2
Operatives (Semiskilled)	23,893	3,637	15.2	18,595	2,373	12.8	5,298	1,264	23.9
Laborers (Unskilled)	1,825	660	36.2	1,438	589	41.0	387	71	18.3
Service workers	2,066	637	30.8	1,563	529	33.8	503	108	21.5
Total	117,033	7,966	6.8	99,474	6,222	6.3	17,559	1,744	9.9

Source: Data in author's possession.

Note: For geographic definitions, see Table 16, p. 32.

large jet engine facility; St. Louis, the home of McDonnell; and Wichita, Kansas, which contains a large facility of Boeing, and the manufacturing facilities of Cessna, Beech, and Lear-Jet. The heaviest Negro concentrations are found in the McDonnell and General Electric plants.

McDonnell, as noted earlier in this study, has long been a practicer of equal employment opportunity. Located near a center of Negro population, although a long commute from the St. Louis North Side, it has made strenuous efforts to recruit Negro employees. The great success of its Phantom jet fighter has enabled it to break down jobs into semiskilled components and has thus enabled it to develop entry jobs that have attracted large numbers of Negro men and women who have previously not worked in industry. McDonnell has also been quite successful in upgrading Negroes. Its long record of Negro employment has facilitated this, for Negroes employed many years ago have been able to work up, or to train for higher jobs. McDonnell's ratio of Negro employees is more than twice that of the industry, with a higher than average percentage in the skilled category.

General Electric likewise has a forceful program of equal opportunity, and has applied it at Evandale where many Negroes are migrants from the South. The result today is that the Evendale plant has a relatively high proportion of Negroes in the skilled categories.

At Wichita, Negro representation in the major plants has lagged, although both Boeing and Beech have made very strenuous efforts to improve minority group work participation. Beech has been quite successful over the years in integrating its minority work force throughout its light plane manufacturing facility. The Negro population of Wichita, 8 percent in 1960, and estimated at about 12 percent today, is of course considerably less than that in the St. Louis or Cincinnati areas.

The most significant aspects of the favorable attitudes and programs in the major Midwest facilities is the high Negro representation in the craftsmen and office and clerical occupational groups. In the former, the Negro percentage in the Midwest region is 6.2, as compared with the 4.6 national average; in the office and clerical group, the Midwest percentage is 3.4; the national, 2.8. Negro females also are much better represented in the Midwest than in the country as a whole. A combination of favorable employer attitudes and policies of long standing, character of work and work mix, and the heavy Negro migration to the area have combined to make the Midwest

TABLE 25. *Aerospace Industry, Employment by Race, Sex, and Occupational Group, West Coast Region, 1966*

Occupational Group	All Employees			Male			Female		
	Total	Negro	Percent Negro	Total	Negro	Percent Negro	Total	Negro	Percent Negro
Officials and managers	35,016	134	0.4	34,615	132	0.4	401	2	0.5
Professionals	96,055	858	0.9	93,561	817	0.9	2,494	41	1.6
Technicians	32,115	679	2.1	27,856	638	2.3	4,259	41	1.0
Sales workers	284	—	—	242	—	—	42	—	—
Office and clerical	68,319	1,824	2.7	23,547	888	3.8	44,772	936	2.1
Craftsmen (Skilled)	73,318	3,831	5.2	69,099	3,490	5.1	4,219	341	8.1
Operatives (Semiskilled)	62,630	8,031	12.8	45,292	5,882	13.0	17,338	2,149	12.4
Laborers (Unskilled)	1,711	353	20.6	1,467	335	22.8	244	18	7.4
Service workers	5,917	1,022	17.3	4,969	896	18.0	948	126	13.3
Total	375,365	16,732	4.5	300,648	13,078	4.3	74,717	3,654	4.9

Source: Data in author's possession.
Note: For geographic definitions, see Table 16, p. 32.

TABLE 26. *Aerospace Industry, Employment by Race, Sex, and Occupational Group, Southern California Region, 1966*

	All Employees			Male			Female		
Occupational Group	Total	Negro	Percent Negro	Total	Negro	Percent Negro	Total	Negro	Percent Negro
Officials and managers	21,056	99	0.5	20,748	97	0.5	308	2	0.6
Professionals	64,600	648	1.0	62,839	612	1.0	1,761	36	2.0
Technicians	18,336	496	2.7	16,067	470	2.9	2,269	26	1.1
Sales workers	271	—	—	236	—	—	35	—	—
Office and clerical	44,284	1,336	3.0	14,744	620	4.2	29,540	716	2.4
Craftsmen (Skilled)	48,342	3,035	6.3	45,412	2,771	6.1	2,930	264	9.0
Operatives (Semiskilled)	43,241	6,557	15.2	29,521	4,788	16.2	13,720	1,769	12.9
Laborers (Unskilled)	1,462	331	22.6	1,235	313	25.3	227	18	7.9
Service workers	4,244	873	20.6	3,517	780	22.2	727	93	12.8
Total	245,836	13,375	5.4	194,319	10,451	5.4	51,517	2,924	5.7

Source: Data in author's possession.

Note: For geographic definitions, see Table 16, p. 32.

aerospace centers among the most favorable in the industry to Negro employment.

The West Coast, and particularly Southern California, ranks with the Midwest as the area giving Negroes the best employment opportunities qualitatively and quantitatively. Total West Coast (Table 25) includes, besides Southern California, the great Boeing plants in Seattle and the various installations near San Jose, south of San Francisco. At Seattle, where only about 5 percent of the population is Negro, Boeing has done extensive recruiting and upgrading and has many Negro engineers and technicians as well as lower-rated personnel. Both Lockheed and United Aircraft in Northern California have extensively recruited and trained Negroes, especially those from the Oakland area.

Southern California (Table 26) has about the same percentage of Negro operatives and craftsmen as the Midwest region, and thus like the Midwest region is ahead of the national average in these important groups. The Negro concentration in the lowest two job categories in Southern California is almost identical with the national average, as is Negro female employment.

In the office and clerical group, Southern California is slightly better (3.0 to 2.8) than the national percentage, but its superiority is greater with the male clerical group. Undoubtedly, the proportion of Negro female office and clerical employees is reduced because of travel and commuting problems between Negro residential areas and plant locations in Southern California.

Southern California is the leading region in the industry, both numerically and in proportion, of Negro officials and managers, professionals, and technicians. Perhaps, like their white counterparts, Negroes in these groups flock to the balmy weather of the area. It is also true, however, that the Southern California industry has had a long record of utilizing Negro personnel in these areas.

Southern California is the headquarters of Lockheed, North American, Douglas, Hughes, Northrop, the Convair Division of General Dynamics, and Aerojet-General, as well as many smaller companies. All are now firmly committed to strong affirmative action, and several like Lockheed, Douglas, and North American have done so for a number of years. If the industry continues to expand its employment in this region, Negroes can expect continued gains.

SOUTHERN DEVELOPMENTS IN THE 1960's

The South (Tables 27-29) offers in some ways a more discouraging picture than other areas, but in other ways one of increasing promise. Table 27, which includes both the Southeast and the Southwest, shows excessively heavy concentrations of Negroes in the lowest two occupational groups—concentrations one and one-half to twice the national average—but underrepresentation in the operative and craftsmen level compared with the national picture. Surprisingly, the salaried groups show representation of Negroes very close to the national average and, in the case of office and clerical, actually superior to the national average. The significance of, and reasons for, these surprising Negro gains in the salaried area can best be explained by examining the data for the Southeast—Table 28.

The data for the South are divided into two groups—Southeast (Table 28) and Southwest (Table 29). To one who is not familiar with developments in the Southeast, the picture presented by Table 28 must come as a great surprise. To be sure, about one-third of the laborers and service workers are Negroes, as compared with less than one-fourth nationally. But Negro representation among the semiskilled operatives is almost identical with that nationally (11.7 to 11.9), and the same is true among craftsmen (4.1 to 4.6). Then one finds that Negro office and clerical employees comprise 4.2 percent of those in the Southeast, but only 2.8 percent of those nationally! Moreover, representation among the officials and managers, professionals, and technicians for Negroes in the Southeast is nearly identical with that nationally.

What has happened in the Southeast is that a number of major aerospace companies have opened facilities, and partially because they have practiced equal employment, and partially under federal government prodding, they have changed employment practices of a region in a major manner. Despite the high skill content of their work, they have done much more in this regard than many other industries, for example, automobiles, which have tended much more to maintain the status quo. Many of these companies have installations at space centers like Huntsville, Alabama, Cape Kennedy, Florida, Bay St. Louis, Mississippi, or Michaud, Louisiana. Others, such as Martin-Marietta or United Aircraft established facilities near these. A third group, Lockheed at Marietta, Georgia, or Avco at Nashville, Tennessee, operated plants which had their genesis in

TABLE 27. *Aerospace Industry, Employment by Race, Sex, and Occupational Group, South Region, 1966*

Occupational Group	All Employees			Male			Female		
	Total	Negro	Percent Negro	Total	Negro	Percent Negro	Total	Negro	Percent Negro
Officials and managers	11,341	35	0.3	11,270	35	0.3	71	—	—
Professionals	30,459	184	0.6	29,984	176	0.6	475	8	1.7
Technicians	10,437	146	1.4	9,779	133	1.4	658	13	2.0
Sales workers	142	—	—	142	—	—	—	—	—
Office and clerical	21,644	658	3.0	9,859	389	3.9	11,785	269	2.3
Craftsmen (Skilled)	23,903	556	2.3	23,478	552	2.4	425	4	0.9
Operatives (Semiskilled)	26,456	2,195	8.3	23,356	1,999	8.6	3,100	196	6.3
Laborers (Unskilled)	541	228	42.1	481	221	45.9	60	7	11.7
Service workers	1,898	674	35.5	1,827	640	35.0	71	34	47.9
Total	126,821	4,676	3.7	110,176	4,145	3.8	16,645	531	3.2

Source: Data in author's possession.
Note: For geographic definitions, see Table 16, p. 32.

TABLE 28. *Aerospace Industry, Employment by Race, Sex, and Occupational Group, Southeast Region, 1966*

Occupational Group	All Employees			Male			Female		
	Total	Negro	Percent Negro	Total	Negro	Percent Negro	Total	Negro	Percent Negro
Officials and managers	6,158	24	0.4	6,126	24	0.4	32	—	—
Professionals	18,221	147	0.8	17,952	141	0.8	269	6	2.2
Technicians	6,669	116	1.7	6,288	106	1.7	381	10	2.6
Sales workers	115	—	—	115	—	—	—	—	—
Office and clerical	12,022	501	4.2	5,259	298	5.7	6,763	203	3.0
Craftsmen (Skilled)	11,441	468	4.1	11,263	465	4.1	178	3	1.7
Operatives (Semiskilled)	11,857	1,383	11.7	10,541	1,253	11.9	1,316	130	9.9
Laborers (Unskilled)	292	92	31.5	236	85	36.0	56	7	12.5
Service workers	722	261	36.1	671	244	36.4	51	17	33.3
Total	67,497	2,992	4.4	58,451	2,616	4.5	9,046	376	4.2

Source: Data in author's possession.

Note: For geographic definitions, see Table 16, p. 32.

TABLE 29. *Aerospace Industry, Employment by Race, Sex, and Occupational Group, Southwest Region, 1966*

Occupational Group	All Employees			Male			Female		
	Total	Negro	Percent Negro	Total	Negro	Percent Negro	Total	Negro	Percent Negro
Officials and managers	5,183	11	0.2	5,144	11	0.2	39	—	—
Professionals	12,238	37	0.3	12,032	35	0.3	206	2	1.0
Technicians	3,768	30	0.8	3,491	27	0.8	277	3	1.1
Sales workers	27	—	—	27	—	—	—	—	—
Office and clerical	9,622	157	1.6	4,600	91	2.0	5,022	66	1.3
Craftsmen (Skilled)	12,462	88	0.7	12,215	87	0.7	247	1	0.4
Operatives (Semiskilled)	14,599	812	5.6	12,815	746	5.8	1,784	66	3.7
Laborers (Unskilled)	249	136	54.6	245	136	55.5	4	—	—
Service workers	1,176	413	35.1	1,156	396	34.3	20	17	85.0
Total	59,324	1,684	2.8	51,725	1,529	3.0	7,599	155	2.0

Source: Data in author's possession.

Note: For geographic definitions, see Table 16, p. 32.

World War II. All of them have brought with them a new urgency for equal employment opportunity and are constantly pushed farther into affirmative action by governmental presence and prodding.

In space center areas, for example, special councils of the major employers conduct training, recruit at Negro schools, scour the areas for potential employees, and otherwise do what they can to increase Negro representation in the plant. Moreover, their programs to upgrade and to train persons have had great success—as the percentage of Negro craftsmen demonstrates.

Special mention needs to be made of the work of Lockheed since 1961. When it took over the huge facility at Marietta, Georgia, near Atlanta, in 1951, it did not eliminate the segregation practices. Then, Lockheed became the first company to join Plans for Progress, and embarked on a vigorous affirmative action program which soon obtained for it the reputation as the region's most active and interested employer of Negroes. Lockheed, already operating the largest facility in the area, has been aided by an expanding business. Its recruiting, training, and upgrading of Negroes are strongly reflected in the data in Table 28, because Lockheed is by far the largest employer in the Southeast.[36]

Negro women lag somewhat in the Southeast, but not in the office and clerical group where their percentage exceeds the national average of Table 19 (3.0 to 2.2). Here again, active recruiting and training of the aerospace companies have produced results and promise continued progress.

If the data for the Southeast show the great strides which have been made and great promise of even greater improvement, those for the Southwest are rather discouraging. Table 29 shows that in this area in 1966, Negroes were most heavily overconcentrated in the bottom two occupational classifications; that they had only one-half the representation among the semiskilled operatives that they hold nationally (5.6 to 11.9); that their share of craftsmen's work was less than 1 percent as compared with 4.6 percent nationally and of office and clerical jobs only 1.6 percent as compared with 2.8 percent nationally; and that in the top three categories, the Southwest also lagged somewhat. Finally, Negro female employees had fewer jobs in the Southwest than in any other region.

36. For studies of Lockheed's policies, see the article by E. G. Mattison, note 19, *supra;* and Gilbert Burck, "A New Business for Business: Reclaiming Human Resources," *Fortune,* Vol. LXXVII (January 1968), pp. 198-199.

There are several reasons for this situation. A few of the southwest plants are located in places like Tucson, Arizona, or White Sands, New Mexico, where few Negroes dwell. These, however, are relatively small, and the major plants of the area are in the Dallas-Fort Worth area of Texas. These plants are now all committed to equal employment opportunity, but they have been slow both to run short of labor and to adopt affirmative action programs. The General Dynamics plant at Fort Worth, which is building the F-111, is now working at capacity, but was not prior to 1967. In 1967, it added more than 8,000 persons to its payroll. Similarly, employment at the former Chance-Vought plant (now a Ling-Temco-Vought facility) rose 6,000 in 1967 and that at Bell Helicopter by a sizable amount also. Particularly General Dynamics and L-T-V began the 1960's with a very low labor force and a huge number of employees with recall rights. The fact that little integration occurred prior to the mid-1960's was thus a joint product of lack of progress in the 1950's combined with a slow build-up in the 1960's.

There are other reasons for the lack of progress in the Southwest as of 1966. Some of the southwest plants did little training; one until recently required six months experience in entry jobs above laborer and service worker, which obviously meant some other company had to do its training and that few Negroes would qualify. Until prodded by the aerospace companies, the schools in the Fort Worth area, especially, do not seem to have provided much incentive or training for Negroes to enter into industry. Unlike the Atlanta, Georgia, area, where a sizable Negro middle class exists and housing is available for Negro professional, business, and other Negro middle-class personnel, the Dallas-Fort Worth area lags in both such a middle class and in proper or even adequate housing. One company in particular believes housing has been a major block in recruiting Negro engineers for its Fort Worth facility.

Progress has been made in the Dallas-Fort Worth area since 1966. Table 30 contains the racial-occupational employment data for the three major companies there in 1967. These data show substantial increases in the percentage of Negroes, and in the craftsmen and operatives categories over the 1966 data found in Table 29. (Table 29 includes data for several small installations not found in Table 30.) Progress is also indicated by the manner in which Fort Worth and Dallas companies have moved to employ hard-core unemployed and to participate in recent months in other programs designed to

TABLE 30. *Aerospace Industry, Employment by Race, Sex, and Occupational Group Three Major Southwest Companies, 1967*

Occupational Group	All Employees			Male			Female		
	Total	Negro	Percent Negro	Total	Negro	Percent Negro	Total	Negro	Percent Negro
Officials and managers	4,895	18	0.4	4,867	18	0.4	28	—	—
Professionals	10,637	28	0.3	10,439	27	0.3	198	1	0.5
Technicians	2,294	17	0.7	2,112	14	0.7	182	3	1.6
Sales workers	21	—	—	21	—	—	—	—	—
Office and clerical	8,738	144	1.6	4,525	103	2.3	4,213	41	1.0
Craftsmen (Skilled)	14,673	261	1.8	14,347	257	1.8	326	4	1.2
Operatives (Semiskilled)	12,714	963	7.6	11,434	888	7.8	1,280	75	5.9
Laborers (Unskilled)	313	127	40.6	271	119	43.9	42	8	19.0
Service workers	748	320	42.8	739	311	42.1	9	9	100.0
Total	55,033	1,878	3.4	48,755	1,737	3.6	6,278	141	2.2

Source: Data in author's possession.

Note: For geographic definitions, see Table 16, p. 32.

improve minority participation in industry. General Dynamics has opened a new facility at San Antonio which is employing hard-core unemployed minorities almost exclusively.

Nevertheless, the Southwest area still lags in the employment of Negroes, both quantitatively and qualitatively, behind other regions in the aerospace industry. Progress is likely to continue, but the slow start will probably cause the area to continue to lag for many years.

UNION IMPACT ON RACIAL POLICIES

Union influence has in general not been the significant factor in aerospace racial policies that it has been on the positive side in such industries as automobiles or meatpacking, or on the negative side, as in such industries as building construction, railroads, or pulp and paper. The two dominant unions in the industry, the International Association of Machinists and Aerospace Workers (IAM) and the United Automobile, Aerospace and Agricultural Implement Workers (UAW) originally avowed very different policies. The IAM, founded in the railroad shops of Atlanta during the latter half of the nineteenth century, at first limited membership to white workers by constitutional provision, and later accomplished the same thing by a secret ritual which pledged members to admit only competent white mechanics.[37]

In the 1930's, the IAM expanded into the aircraft industry. During World War II, its anti-Negro ritual became a source of embarrassment to its top officials, but not till the late 1940's was it repealed. In some cases, IAM union policies proved a bar to Negro employment in the industry during World War II, but in most cases the IAM did not have a compulsory union membership contract and therefore could not adversely affect Negro employment.

In recent years, the IAM attitude on race is basically a passive one. Locals of the IAM are very independent, with the international exercising only limited interference. As a result, there is little or no affirmative action in support of Negro employment and no national union interference when local unions either drag their feet, or oppose affirmative action programs.[38]

The UAW has had a militant program of equal opportunity for many years. In aerospace, it has supported company programs, but

37. For background on the IAM, and its racial policies, see Northrup, *Organized Labor and the Negro,* pp. 8, 206-208.
38. See Burck, *op. cit.,* p. 198.

at the local union level, this support varies considerably. Unlike the situation in both automobiles and agricultural implements, Negroes comprise only a small part of the membership in the aerospace industry, and have not been able to exert influences in local unions as they have in these other industries. Consequently, although most managements feel that the UAW has given sound support to programs aimed at Negro advancement, it is also true that Negroes play a very minor role in local unions, have few offices above shop steward, and seem generally to the author to be much more inactive than in the automobile industry.[39]

There have been some rank-and-file Negro rumblings against union lack of leadership in the industry. A CORE (Congress of Racial Equality) led group picketed the UAW and North American in the Los Angeles area in 1966, claiming inadequate promotions for Negroes. Generally, however, such demonstrations have been rare, especially since in recent years there has been a great upward movement of Negroes.

In aerospace, the dynamics of racial policies do not seem to be radically influenced by unions. The companies have taken the lead, as they have in employee relations generally,[40] and the unions, although occasionally challenging, supporting, or encouraging, have been the followers. Neither the official indifference of the IAM, nor the loud affirmance of the UAW, seem to have had any decisive effects. Union-management seniority clauses are not aimed at hindering Negro upgrading, and as in the case of Lockheed in Georgia, attempts of local unions to obtain discriminatory seniority provisions have not been successful. Hence seniority clauses do not seem to have hindered Negro job movement. Moreover, job bidding, which is widely used, permits considerable movement within the plant.

GOVERNMENT POLICIES

The government is the aerospace industry's big customer, and government pressure is always a factor that aerospace companies must consider. There can be no doubt that the affirmative action plans which are so prominent in the industry stem from heavy (often heavy-handed) government pressure which motivates employers and keeps

39. A comparison may be found in Northrup, *The Negro in the Automobile Industry*.
40. On this point, see Harold M. Levinson, *Determining Forces in Collective Wage Bargaining* (New York: John Wiley & Sons, Inc., 1966), Chapter 2.

the problem in the forefront and constantly pushes the industry to take further affirmative action. But the government is not a single dimensioned pressure force. The government is also the customer, and it is the policeman. As customer, it demands, as it should, zero defect work. Life is involved and quality of workmanship cannot be compromised. The industry has to certify the capability of workmen on many jobs. Social programs are admirable, but there is no substitute for experience and ability. Affirmative action can go only so far, and educational, cultural, attitudinal deficiencies cannot be either glossed over or overcome quickly. The unfortunate plain fact is that the higher the qualifications which are required, the fewer Negroes are qualified and the more difficult it is to gain qualifications by short-run training or educational programs.

Much of the aerospace work is under tight security. Jail or arrest records at one time automatically meant clearance denials. Given the facts of city slums and Negro-police relations, this was a powerful bar to Negro advancement, or even employment, in the industry.

Now a more sophisticated approach is the rule. Arrest records are scrutinized and the minor infractions discounted. It appears government security and equal opportunity pressures are today more synchronized in approach than formerly.

There is now the danger that the government may push companies too far in liberalizing employment policies. Some in the industry are quite concerned about sabotage and poor workmanship. The pressures on both sides are great, but it should be reiterated that overly zealous minority group employment programs should certainly not be allowed to compromise workmanship standards in this industry. Yet the fact remains that government pressure has historically been a prime motivating force in obtaining increased employment opportunities for Negroes, and it is likely to continue. The results must be considered salutary.

A significant result of government pressure also is the aid which it gives to managers who greatly desire to increase minority employment. The result has been continued social engineering in developing training and motivational programs and a resultant increase in employment and upgrading of Negroes. The aerospace companies now have considerable experience in training those once considered too unskilled to apply—certainly a gain in itself. Of course, only when jobs are broken down by relatively large-scale production can employees so limited be utilized. Fortuitously, the drive for equal employment opportunity has coincided not only with a tremendous expansion of employment in the industry—but an expansion which has been concentrated during the 1965-1967 period in the manned aircraft portion of the industry which can utilize much less skilled labor than can missile or space vehicle development and manufacturing. A downturn in this segment of the industry would have a most adverse impact on Negro aerospace employment.

CHAPTER VI.

Some Problems of Equal Opportunity

The recruitment of large numbers of Negroes into aerospace plants has not been without its problems of adjustment and other difficulties. Excessive absenteeism, tardiness, turnover, learning to live under factory discipline, and slum habits brought into the plant have all been problems, and are discussed with other issues in this section.

IMPACT ON WHITE EMPLOYEES

Unlike the automobile industry in which Negroes comprise either a majority, or a very significant minority of many plants, Negroes remain a small minority in nearly all aerospace facilities. Consequently, there seems to have been little impact on the white labor market. In some industries or plants, where a sizeable portion of Negroes has been employed, whites no longer seek employment there, but no instance of this has been found in aerospace. There are jobs in the South, janitor, for example, in which it has been customary for generations to employ only Negroes. It is difficult there still today to find a white man who will accept such employment, or if he does, remain on the job.

Recent attempts to encourage the building of plants in the slums have led Avco and Aerojet-General to establish facilities in such areas which are, or will be, entirely manned by Negroes. Although this is segregation, it has been both welcomed by Negro leaders and encouraged by the federal government. Time will tell where such approaches to Negro employment problems are viable while at the same time the federal government and Negro leaders attack all vestiges of segregation in other industrial facilities. Moreover, slum-located plants have yet to prove their economic viability. Such plans do, however, reach Negroes who might otherwise not receive any opportunity or training.

The combination of many new Negro employees and large numbers of females in aerospace plants has not been without its problems. Mixed dating or companionship seems to aggravate relations between the races about as much as anything. Alleged passes at white women, or mash notes directed to them, by Negro men have elicited a much larger number and proportion of complaints on the part of women employees than the aerospace companies usually have as a result of men and women being in the same plant. Whether this is because Negroes are more direct in their propositioning, or whether white women are more apt to complain because the approach is made by a Negro, is not clear from the evidence. It has, however, been a problem, and does concern many personnel executives because of its implications for trouble.

EFFICIENCY AND TURNOVER

Of one thing, every aerospace management contacted agrees—the rate of absenteeism, tardiness, and turnover of Negro employees is substantially higher than that of whites. Few detailed studies are available to support these assertions, but the unanimity of opinion and the little evidence available all point in that direction. In one company, 4,052 Negroes were hired in one year, but only 1,509 remained at the end of the twelve months. This turnover was more than three times that of whites for the same period. In a second concern over a six-month period, 11.3 percent of the hires and 10 percent of the terminations were Negroes.

Many other companies cited data for short periods, but nearly always they pointed in the direction of turnover two or three times as high for Negroes. Several reasons were adduced for these facts. The highest turnover group were younger Negroes without any industrial experience. Industrial discipline was a new phenomenon to them. "Man," said one, to a Midwest concern, "you mean 8 to 5 *every* day!" Used to picking up odd jobs for a while, hustling numbers, or doing other facets of slum area income-producing activity, steady work is a radical change and not one to which some could easily adapt.

The great exception to this rule was the mature Negro woman, 25 to 35 years of age, often with a family to support. Repeatedly, white supervisors, including often those who originally opposed hiring Negro women, sang their praises as diligent, hard-working people who could be counted upon to work hard and stay on the job. The strong role that Negro women play in family life, and often as breadwinner, and the great responsibility thrust upon them, seem to have conditioned them to accept the rigors of factory work and to apply themselves diligently to it.

Even here there are sad exceptions. Training for entry jobs in aerospace is usually at wages in the neighborhood of $1.75 per hour. Progression beyond that is rapid, but one has to believe that progress is both possible and worthwhile. One major company found it was losing Negro women trainees after the first paycheck. Investigation showed that take-home pay of the trainees and welfare payments to women with several children were not too different in amount. The fact that the wage progression would go steadily upward was not enough to offset the debilitating effect of our self-defeating aid to dependent children program.

The same factors which contribute to the high turnover rate of Negroes also contribute to their higher rate of tardiness and absenteeism. Inexperience in industry, poor educational backgrounds, lack of motivation as a result of lack of belief in or experience with equal opportunity, are all factors. In addition, the long distances which many Negroes have to commute undoubtedly add to their problems in getting to work on time and regularly.

EFFICIENCY AND GOVERNMENT PRESSURE

Government policy must be credited with a large role in motivating employers and in keeping the significance of the problem to the forefront. As already noted, however, there is a fundamental conflict between social programs to aid the downtrodden and the need for zero defect work. Many companies feel that they are being pushed dangerously far to hire marginal employees. The line between hourly qualifying employees and those whose utilization could prove disastrous is a fine one. A number of concerns have greatly added to their inspection staffs in order to offset the utilization of increasing numbers of marginal employees, many of whom are Negroes.

In some areas, the state of the labor market is such that only marginal employees of either race are available. The satisfaction of several employers with Negro women represents, in part, the pleasant surprise to many operating personnel that there remained a relatively untouched group in the labor market who worked above the marginal level. The industry, however, is caught between the pressures for social progress and the need for zero defects. That the latter must prevail seems obvious. But the line is not always clear where conflict between the two programs exists, or whether the problem is really a basic labor shortage and the availability only of marginal workers, many of whom are Negroes.

One other aspect of government pressure should be noted. The availability of appeal to the government for Negro workers who feel aggrieved is not unknown to many. As in the case of labor relations, where the employee may file a grievance because he was disciplined, or not promoted, or for other reasons, so the Negro may do likewise, but he is more likely, if he believes race a factor, to file his case with a state or federal agency like the Equal Employment Opportunity Commission rather than to utilize the white employee controlled grievance procedure. Often as in the case of labor grievances, the grievant has a good case. More often, however, the real cause is something else—inefficiency, poor workmanship, or bad behavior, with the worst offender the most likely to file a case. That this causes employer anguish and white employee resentment is obvious. It takes time, effort, and great patience, and will be a factor in employee relations for years to come. But it has developed considerable resentment in some plants where white employees feel that some supervisors are afraid to discipline Negroes lest they have to defend themselves in investigations by government agencies. Charges of double standards because of race are not new, but now the charge is that Negroes in some plants are favored.

SOME PERSPECTIVES

Despite the great problems of adjustment, thousands of Negroes are learning valuable skills in the aerospace industry. They are now better prepared as workers to maintain their economic well-being and as citizens to care for themselves and their families. A substantial bank of skills has been added to the human capital in America by increased Negro employment in the aerospace industry. The difficulties, tribulations, and failures are relatively minor compared to this all-important accomplishment. Hopefully, the longer the plant tenure of the new Negro aerospace employees, the less will be the problems.

CHAPTER VII.

Determinants of Industry Policy

In the course of this study, a number of factors have been pointed out which have contributed to the racial employment policies of the aerospace industry. These and others should be noted again in the following concluding remarks.

THE DEMAND FOR LABOR

As in most industries, Negroes have made their greatest gains in the aerospace industry in times of full employment, and by the very nature of the industry, this means in times of war. The barriers were broken during World War II; serious upgrading occurred during the Korean War; and now the impetus of Vietnam, on top of the space program, has further expanded opportunities for development and promotion. But this has not been a smooth transition. Huge layoffs occurred after World War II, after the Korean armistice, and again in 1958, affecting the whole industry. Depending on the ebb and flow of government procurement, one company expands, another contracts, a plant may be abandoned or opened up.

As the last hired and the most recently upgraded, Negroes have found that their gains were washed out time and again. Yet, each time, as a result of the gains of the previous cycle, further gains were made in both numbers and in terms of occupational advancement; today's have been the greatest, and tomorrow's may be greater still, with again progress uneven, and many setbacks as the industry or some companies ebb and flow.

THE JOB STRUCTURE

Of fundamental importance in the industry is the job structure and the high professional content thereof. With professionals and skilled craftsmen the largest two occupational groups, and with Negroes disproportionately unrepresented in both groups, Negro advancement in the industry is certain to be retarded for many years. The unfortunate fact is that the higher the qualifications which are required, the fewer Negroes are qualified and the more difficult it is to gain qualification by short-run training or educational programs. As has been stressed, the aerospace industry must require skill and educational attainments that few Negroes possess, and there cannot be legitimate compromise with these requirements. Acquiring skills and education is a time-consuming process, so that upward job movement in this industry will continue to lag as long as the Negro educational and skill gap endures. Moreover, because of inexperience in industry, lack of help in setting goals, and the difficulty of breaking with the past, progress and upward job movement are made more difficult.

Past discrimination is difficult to overcome. Where Negroes are employed only for laboring jobs, they often lack background, capacity, and motivation to grasp new opportunities. It is expecting too much for a man who knew that he would always be a laborer ever to believe that he may be promoted if he takes training. Forty acres and a mule can be promised once too often to be taken seriously.

Opportunities appear greater in new plants. Rigidities are not set, custom can be violated without resistance of existing personnel, and past mistakes avoided. New plants may, however, be farther from cities, the new centers of Negro population, and here lack of public transportation and housing discrimination curtail Negro job and job advancement opportunities.

GOVERNMENT PRESSURE

Government pressure has been, and remains, a strong motivational force. With the government so large a customer, the industry cannot afford not to cooperate in all affirmative action programs. The government has not only opened up jobs, but has in effect in many cases pushed for what is close to outright preference for Negroes, and the industry has not only gone along, but often, first under pressure, endorsed the programs and activities and followed through diligently, and then having been committed, developed newer and more far-reaching affirmative action programs.

Yet even the most affirmative of actions cannot create jobs where there are none or fill skills that do not exist. The work must be there or the job openings are not. Layoffs will, as noted, have a profound effect on Negro employment in the industry.

Government pressure, moreover, is multidimensional as was discussed in detail on pages 76-78, and the needs of zero defects and security cannot be ignored.

SENIORITY AND UNIONISM

Because of the significance of skill and training in the industry, seniority has not been as significant as in some industries for promotion. Generally, seniority districts are broad enough so as not to interfere with opportunities for Negroes, and widespread use of job bidding further opens up potential advancement opportunities.

Unionism in the industry has not been a strong negative or positive factor in Negro job advancement. The UAW is more positive than the IAM, which originally was avowedly discriminatory, but is no more, yet is at best, passive. The UAW has not had the strong positive influence in this industry that it has had in the automobile industry where its position in all employee relations matters is much more powerful.

LOCATIONAL AND REGIONAL FACTORS

The location of aerospace companies in suburban or outer county areas, combined with the concentration of Negroes in cities, lack of good public urban transportation, and housing discrimination all tend to make getting to work in aerospace for Negroes a difficult problem and one which reduces Negro participation in the industry.

On a regional basis, the existence of large aerospace plants throughout the country has been generally salutary. Aerospace led the way in opening up new jobs to Negroes in the Far West during World War II, and in the Southeast in recent years. Its recent progress in the Southwest is especially noteworthy on a qualitative basis. The Southwest area lags considerably behind the Southeast in the utilization of Negro labor in this industry. Plants in this area are behind the trends in the industry despite diligent, but late efforts to improve Negro employment patterns there.

MANAGERIAL POLICY

Management is now committed to the full use of Negro labor in the industry. The needs and pressures are such that this policy will certainly not be turned back. From an industry which was once known for its extreme antagonism to Negro employment it has become as active as any in affirmative action programs. The reasons are an amalgam of what has been written above.

Of course, within the industry there exists a wide range of views and opinions among companies on questions of equal opportunity and affirmative action. It is fair to say, however, that most managements have a strong moral commitment to equal opportunity, but varying degrees of belief or support of the different affirmative action programs. Dealing as they do, primarily with government officials and air transport concerns, they do not feel the direct impact of the consuming public. Yet they are, and must be, very sensitive to public opinion and to their public image. For even the few who may be dubious about equal employment have a clear understanding of the necessity of proceeding to get the job accomplished as well as they can. The progress made, and the commitment which governmental and company policies have brought about augur well for the future of Negroes in the industry.

Index